RFD
Vermont

Marguerite Hurrey Wolf

The New England Press
Shelburne, Vermont

The New England Press
P.O. Box 575
Shelburne, Vermont 05482

Library of Congress Catalog Card Number: 87-62757
ISBN: 0-933050-55-0

Cover illustration by Paul O. Boisvert

Printed by Queen City Printers Inc., Burlington, Vermont
PRINTED IN THE UNITED STATES OF AMERICA

RFD Vermont

Contents

RFD Vermont

North of Megalopolis,
A Foreword

North of WHAT? Never mind the latitude. It is the multitude I prefer to keep at more than arm's length – the lines of slow-moving traffic, acres of concrete, shopping malls and condominiums.

When we first came to Vermont in 1948, northern Vermont was relaxed and rural. There really were more cows than people, no traffic lights, no parking garages and you could park in front of the store of your choice on Church Street in Burlington. Of course there was no interstate, limited shopping, and very few good restaurants. Gourmet was a noun, the antithesis of gourmand. Williston Road was shaded by elm trees, the Deslauriers' farm was on the site of the present Sheraton Inn and Al's French Fries was the only fast-food establishment.

I have to admit that the tentacles of urbanization are reaching out from Vermont's small cities. Our village of

Jericho Center is becoming a bedroom community, a suburb rather than a farming community. But with our nearest neighbor barely visible through the trees we still stoutly maintain that we live in the country. Certainly there are few urban amenities. We live on a dirt road, albeit better maintained than the city streets. Our water comes from our own well and we carry our own refuse to the town sanitary (what DO they mean by that?) landfill. We can still see an occasional deer, a fox or a flying squirrel, a pileated woodpecker and far too many woodchucks for our taste.

It is an environment I enjoy, living in alternating harmony or battle with the seasons and writing about the pleasures and pitfalls of life north of megalopolis.

"Are you still writing?" I am frequently asked, the tone implying that I should have outgrown it by now. The look of surprise when I admit to this aberration makes me want to ask, "Are you still eating?"

I write for the same reason—because I enjoy doing it for the most part, and because it nourishes me. Every writer I know is essentially an autobiographer, whether or not they use the first person. Even fiction bears the imprint of the author's interests and interpretation.

I was tempted to call this book *Jericho Journal* partly because of the alliteration and the fact that it is widely believed that every writer does or should keep a journal. You are told that in all writing courses and conferences. But while I admire the journals of May Sarton or Lee Huntington, they are really poets rather than journalists. The garden variety of journals have a tendency to turn into weather reports and I'm not sure all of our weather deserves that much publicity.

But the earth does turn whether or not we are aware of it. I'm not. I think of it as flat and stationary in spite of Galileo and Copernicus. When you live in a multiple-season climate, your life is clearly defined by the seasons. Of course in Vermont it isn't four seasons. We have at least nine, pre-spring (April), real spring (May), spring-like summer (June), real summer (July), hint of fall (August), Indian summer (September), real fall (October), early winter (November) and real winter from then on through far too much of March.

When I look up a word in the dictionary I invariably get diverted by another word and nearly forget the one I was looking for. That's what happens when I try to keep a journal. Something as ordinary as doing the laundry will trigger a reminiscence or observation that drifts far afield. You'll just have to trust me that if there are moments when a peripatetic sheep or the undulating flight of a goldfinch shove the weather off the page it's not likely to halt the revolution of the earth and I'll try to jump back on again at the appropriate seasons.

The cast of characters here is mostly the same as in my previous books except that some of us are changing. You would only notice it in our grandsons, Patrick, Peter and Morgan who now, at ages eleven, nine, and six, are big boys, and in the grandparents, George and I, who are shrinking. Our two daughters, Patty and Debbie, and their husbands, Tage Strom and Steve Page, seem to be frozen in time. They simply improve with age.

The scene for the most part is our rocky and wooded 15 acres in Jericho, Vermont which have exacted blood, sweat, and love from us for thirty-eight years.

The theme is expressed in a letter Thomas Jefferson wrote

to James Madison in 1793.

"The motion of my blood no longer keeps time with the tumult of the world. It leads me to seek happiness in the lap and love of my family, the society of my neighbors and my books, in the wholesome occupation of my farms and my affairs in an interest or affection for every bud that opens."

In Praise of
Country Living

It used to happen more often when we first moved from New York City to Vermont thirty-five years ago, three years after we first purchased the old homestead. Friends from the city, sitting on our porch sipping a nice cold drink would ask, "What do you DO in the country?" My silent response was that we rarely did what they were doing at that moment. We almost never sit on the deck in the sun. We eat on the porch in the summer, but we don't just sit there because we don't have any time from mid-April to mid-November to just sit.

True, we do sit in the winter, indoors. We read, watch tv, write all sort of things, drink, and eat, all while in a sedentary position. Our friends from the city do that too. But we also feed the animals, the birds, the people and the wood stove. We move large amounts of snow from paths and driveway to snowbanks on either side with the snowblower

(George) or shovels and broom (me) and pray that it won't blow back in right away. We shop, cook, go to meetings and classes, or appointments just like our urban friends.

So what's the big difference? There really isn't any. I think they are asking, "*Why* do you live in the country?" What are the rewards for a life that they see only as less convenient.

One plus is that it is cheaper, but that's not what keeps us rural. Taxes are lower, somewhat, and we raise a good part of our food (but not for economic reasons).

I'll admit that there are a few days each year, in January or February, when I agree with an old friend who said bluntly, "I don't see why you make life so hard for yourselves."

If "the electric" goes off or the plumbing springs a leak, life is hard. But we have Cecil Spalding up the road—an amiable neighbor and plumber — and a generator which is a reluctant starter but a psychological comfort. The only real difference between managing without electricity in the country and in the city is that our water is coaxed up from the well to our house by electricity. In town, water supply and pumps are the city's problem, not yours. But if you live in the city you still can't turn on your typewriter, electric stove, vacuum cleaner, lights, or toaster without power. True, you probably don't use wood for heat in the city except for an occasional fire in the fireplace (which warms the chimney and the air above your roof more than it does the room). But we are not dependent on our wood stove. We have electric baseboard heat which we keep at a minimum because it has become so expensive, but even with the power off our gas heater and the wood stove can keep this small house warm.

As far as snow removal is concerned, the only time it was

a problem was when George had a leg injury. We had to call on Cary Todriff to plow out the driveway. He was here by 7:30 A.M. each time and had our driveway clear in five minutes. I'll bet that beats the city services for promptness and reliability. Steve and Debbie came over, and while they shovelled and blew the path to the barn, Morgan rearranged the edges with his little bulldozer, with great concentration and appropriate sound effects.

Granted that while the benefits of country living are fewer in the winter months (unless you are skiers), it still is lovely to look out on a winter wonderland of pristine fields and evergreens that look like Christmas cards. When our girls were toddlers in New York City, I used to stuff them into their snowsuits as soon as there was a snowfall and make a dash for Central Park so they could have a few minutes of playing in clean snow before it turned to gray slush. Here we are surrounded by clean snow for four to five months. As soon as it gets a little crusty or dirty it snows again, giving us a fresh smooth surface to ski on, play in, or look at. It is so much with us that by March I tire of it, but it is better than the icy or slushy city streets. I can remember stepping off the curb in New York into eight inches of slush and icy water. And in Boston we had bouts of freezing rain, sudden blindness when we were driving, and the "skidiest" of all surfaces.

Mud season is something else and probably the less said about it the better. Like labor pains it is intermittent and you know that something nice is about to happen. If you have several miles of "unimproved" road between your home and the paved road you may feel that you are living on an island in a sea of mud any time from mid-March to mid-

April. We are only one mile from the paved road and our road crews do a heroic job of scraping and filling and dumping gravel, but when the frost comes up out of the ground in early spring even the paved roads buckle and crack and "Frost Heaves" signs blossom before the pussy willows. Never ignore them. Even if you don't see the bump it is lying in wait for you. It may only mean a roller-coaster swell or two favored by small grandsons, but it can also mean neck-snapping, muffler-dislocating bumps best approached in a lower than usual gear. But I can't give city dwellers the advantage at this season when I remember the potholes which make a moonscape of city streets. And they are far more unexpected and treacherous to cars and lower backs than frost heaves.

Spring is splendid, city or country. We just see more of it in the country. Fuzzy gray-green ferns hunch up along every roadside and mists of shadbush blossoms are caught among the trees. What do we do in spring in the country? We enjoy it, every minute of it. We plant the garden with the sun warm on our backs. We hang the laundry outdoors where it flaps noisily in the wind. There is something new to be discovered every day—a robin's nest being built in a crotch in the pine tree, a patch of wood anemones across the road, crimson osier wands near the brook, and the weeping willows glowing with golden light. I like the smell of the wet, brown leaf mulch that I lift off the daffodil beds revealing the first anemic-looking spears. Some spears have impaled a leaf and wear it like a collar. The crocuses look like Easter eggs scattered on the lawn and the pussy willows next to the mailbox are covered with golden pollen. When we had geese in early April I would find a huge goose egg now and then in the ridiculous nest they preferred, which was an old tire filled with straw. A goose egg is so big compared to a chicken egg that it seems like it must have been laid by a pterodactyl, or at least an ostrich.

What I do in the country in the spring is sniff and explore and welcome everything that emerges except the blackflies and those dive bombers, the deerflies. A lot of unpleasant things are said about dandelions, but I love to see whole fields spangled with their living gold.

In the summer no one questions the pleasures of life in the country. A lot of my time is spent either in the vegetable garden or in cooking its products for the same curious guests from the city. But I don't begrudge the time in the garden. It is my exercise, my psychiatrist, and my recreation in the literal sense. I am recreated by it. There is nothing like hoeing the corn to work off a wave of anxiety or frustration. Unlike many other activities you can not only see the results of your labor but you can smell, touch, and eat them too. If I were blind I would still like to feel the tendrils of the pea vines, the satiny roundness of a tomato and smell the dill, parsley, and onions.

Then in the fall all of nature seems to build up into a crescendo of sensation, the pleasure of walking up a country road bordered by blazing maples, the crunch and smell of ripe leaves underfoot, and the various fragrances of apples, chrysanthemums and pickle-making. The fall is slightly bittersweet because of its evanescence. It really is no more fleeting than spring or summer, but it presages a long sleep that resembles death, while the evanescence of spring is the promise of abundant life.

What we do in the country is touch the strength of

wildness and become strengthened ourselves from its nearness.

In *Earth Shine*, Anne Lindbergh wrote, "Immersion in wilderness life, like immersion in the sea, may return civilized man to a basic element from which he sprang and with which he has now lost contact."

That's what I want to hold on to.

Pats and Pans

Some of the fringe benefits of having a book or two published are very pleasant. The members of your immediate family discover that your range of usefulness reaches farther than the stove, sink and taxi service. Your children are surprised and somewhat embarrassed by this, but then when your children are teenagers they often are embarrassed by their mother no matter what she does.

People you've never heard of write letters saying that they have enjoyed your books. Women's clubs ask you to speak and a book club chooses your book for their list. You begin to think that while your words may not be immortal at least they are alive.

So it is just as well that this new complacency is shaken periodically by the head-shrinking comments of the young. Not your own. You are used to that. Strange little faces with gaps in their teeth when they smile up at you. There is nothing like the candid comments of first- and second-graders to keep you humble.

When I talked to Debbie's class at the Flynn School, the children were puzzled by the fact that I am their teacher's mother.

"No, you're her *grandmother*," one insisted. "You have to be because you are the grandmother in her family. She has a mister and he's the Daddy and so you are her grandmother."

O.K., but I'm having enough trouble with aging without being called my daughter's grandmother! If Debbie's real grandmothers were alive they would be over one hundred years old. That hardly puts a spring in my step. Another little girl said, "Don't you wish Mrs. Page was a little girl again and then you'd be a mother instead of a grandmother? Grandmothers die. Mine did."

My confidence was restored by a letter a little girl from another school wrote, "You weren't as boring as I had expected." And one brief moment of glory came when a little boy said, "Jeezum Crow. Your talk was better than recess!"

Another head-shrinking experience is being on display at a bookstore. The aim is to sell books of course and that sometimes happens but not as often as the bookstore owner, or you, might enjoy. I am not famous enough to draw a crowd. As the late Stephen Greene once said, "No sex, no violence but a h _____ good evening's entertainment." People don't stare at me on the street unless I fall down on the ice.

But when you are on display at a bookstore you are visible but apparently deaf. One lady stopped a few feet away, studied me from various angles and remarked to her companion, "She doesn't look like an author, does she? She looks like a regular person." Other comments have been, "I don't believe a doctor's wife loads pigs. She probably made it up." "Come on. You don't want her autograph. She isn't anybody." One young man picked up one of my books and asked, "Is it any good?"

One little boy relieved the tension by coming right up and saying "Hello!" (Just as if I were a "regular person".) Then he went on to say, "I know about another author. He was a king and had a round table where the knights sat after work." How do you like that, Guinevere?

Spring

Who says the new year starts in January? Well, the calendars and the Internal Revenue Service do, but they are primarily concerned with numbers. I'm not. During my school, college, and teaching years the new year started for me in September, and since I've been a country person my year begins with the first intimations of spring.

In the north country the arrival of spring and the first day of spring do not coincide. Verdant spring may be two months away but the first portents are anticipated and savored with an excitement unknown farther south. So some night in March when a winter-hungry raccoon pries open the wires of our suet holder and makes off with the suet we know that spring is stirring and that the chipmunk's internal alarm clock will soon rouse him from his nest. One year we saw a chipmunk in February but he must have misread his early warning signals. In March the temperature

16

often drops to zero at night but may reach thirty degrees during the day, and there is noticeable warmth in the sun. Icicles are melting and dripping from the eaves.

Ice shanties are being hauled off the ice on the lake and loaded onto pickup trucks. Some pussy willows are out. Dorcas Houston brought me a bunch of her big pink French ones. Our smaller native ones won't fuzz out for a couple of more weeks. Our bird population has been sparse the last few years—few evening grosbeaks or purple finches—and it's been years since we've entertained a flock of redpolls.

After the comparative silence of winter when the snow sifts down as softly as a whisper and even the turbulence of our brook is muffled to a mere gurgle under its stalactites of ice, spring announces itself boisterously.

The brook pushes at the creaking ice and bursts free in a roaring torrent, exulting in its freedom. We are awakened by the staccato ping-ping-ping of a flicker drumming on our metal chimney pipe. If the chimney isn't his choice, it is the siding on the house. His enthusiasm for proclaiming his territory and declaring himself an eligible bachelor is not shared by us at 5:00 A.M.

But it's a sound of spring, and once the flicker has his bailiwick established he'll get on with quieter business. As I walk out to the barn a crow flaps heavily overhead cawing hoarsely, and a great avalanche of snow skids down the metal barn roof and lands with a plop inconveniently in front of the barn door.

In the years when we hung a few pails on one or two of our old maples, as soon as you drove in the spile you could hear the pling, pling of the sap in the metal buckets. Now we have plastic bags and the drip is barely audible.

The first few times I heard a ruffed grouse drumming I had no idea who or what was making that noise. It sounded just like an aged motor starting up laboriously, whump — — whump — — whump — whump — whump, accelerating rapidly until it was almost a continuous sound. Now I welcome his mating invitation to any female grouse within earshot and wish I could see him perched on some prominent log pumping his wings to produce his unique love call. I've never been able to find him in action. The sound and the bird are both elusive.

But of course the true sound of spring in Vermont, the assurance that winter has receded for seven months, is heard on the first evening when the peepers chime out their sleigh bell chorus. Then you know that spring has arrived. Even if your bones and the thermometer warn that you may be overly optimistic and you can see and smell it only in the most fleeting glimpses and ephemeral scents, you can hear it loud and clear.

It's really spring!

March and April

March 21. I saw five robins on a lawn and one at the very top of our large maple. He was silhouetted so I couldn't see his russet breast, but his shape was robin-like and he was singing robinese very definitely, a rising and falling caroling that is hard to translate into words. "Cheerily, cheerily," come close. It is still cold for the end of March, right at freezing, thirty-two degrees, with a mean north wind.

April 9. There is still a dusting of snow on the ground but the green spikes of the crocuses are poking through the snow. Snowdrops are in bloom. This is their third appearance. First they came through the crusty crystalized snow. Then twice they were buried by several inches of soft sugar snow. But their bells are ringing inaudible fairy music today.

April 11. Planted some red onion sets in the little salad garden between the old house and the barn. A nice warm sunny day, full of vernal promise. We have one red squirrel who is very red—red fox red—and another one who is more grey than red, but he is definitely not a grey squirrel. That one is an old friend. He has a scar across his back—from the talons of a hawk?—and he has come to the feeder for at least three years, maybe more. The chicadees are not flocking to the feeders as frequently as a month ago, but they are still our regulars along with the blue jays and the downy and hairy woodpeckers.

April 14. At the side of the garage, near a stack of fence poles, there is a mound of fresh earth, a good-sized pile, enough to fill a bushel basket. At one end of the pile there is a hole, the entrance to a tunnel. It would look like the work of a woodchuck except that the hole is only as big around as a golf ball. No woodchuck big enough to move that small mountain of earth could possibly fit through that entrance. Our red squirrels are primarily arboreal. They use little tunnels through the snow and through some earth beneath our bird feeders, but they are not real burrowers. One book on mammals says that a chipmunk does not leave a mound of earth at the entrance to his burrow. So much for definitive statements about what animals never do. I *saw* a chipmunk come out of the little tunnel yesterday.

April 23. My birthday, a lovely sunny day with the temperature up to seventy degrees! Poked around in the asparagus bed. The soil is so wet in the garden that I could pull up dandelion plants, long root and all, very satisfying because some roots are a foot long and if you break them off they start up all over again. No sign of asparagus tips peeking through yet, but the chives are flourishing and tightly convoluted rosy leaves of rhubarb are up a couple of inches.

I think a pair of blue jays are househunting in a white pine west of the house. They are so wary and suspicious, paranoid really. They keep looking over their shoulders, on guard for impending disasters. When they start to build a nest they go through a complicated maneuver, never going directly to the nest site, but hopping from a lower branch to a higher one on the opposite side of the tree, gradually spiralling up the tree on what Owen Pettingill Jr. calls "an invisible staircase." But today I couldn't see any nest building.

April 25. Went to the Lang farm in Essex today to get two baby pigs. The large airfreight dog carrier that Howard Taylor has supplied us with on more-or-less permanent loan makes transporting baby animals so much easier. We used to bring baby pigs home in a couple of grain bags which was very unsettling for both the pigs and us. They could work a small breathing hole into an aperture big enough for a pink snout or a leg to wiggle out and their squeals of protest were unnerving. But now they just ride standing up with plenty of room to snuffle and move about. There is nothing funnier or more compact than a six-week-old piglet. They are so shy when we first unload them into their pen, twinkling in tiptoes to the farthest corner and trying to burrow down into the shavings with only a moist snout and a shoe-button eye peeking out.

April 27. The amethyst tips of the asparagus are up an inch. It's a long wait for those first spears. We don't really begin to eat asparagus until mid-May but just seeing those first tips is exciting. Lettuce in the salad garden is just through the earth and was being inspected by a white-throated sparrow.

April 28. Patrick Strom's birthday. Patrick is our oldest

21

grandson. His first birthdays were in Finland. His seventh and eighth were in Denmark and his ninth, tenth, and eleventh in Ambler, Pennsylvania. It's a nice time of year for a birthday. Mine is a few days earlier and I've always been happy to have a spring birthday. I know what it was like in their garden in Denmark, fruit trees in bloom and daffodils and tulips everywhere. Even in Vermont you can begin to believe in spring towards the end of April. Our daffodils are in bloom and we eat out on the porch for the first time. The asparagus and rhubarb are up about three inches and I have a hard time controlling my desire to pick them. The first taste of spring is better than the old spring tonic, sulphur and molasses.

May 15. Finally saw the blue jays' nest! It is well hidden on a branch of one of the white pines, maybe twelve feet from the ground, out at the end of the branch where the tufts of needles are dense. The only way I can see it is to stand almost under it and look straight up. From another angle I can see mama jay's head so she must be incubating the eggs now. I haven't heard a sound from either parent, though I often see them. They were their usual raucous selves until a week ago but now they have a secret they don't want anyone to discover. In contrast, two robins are building a nest in another pine tree and they scold me loudly whenever I walk near the spot. I've seen them fly down to the garden, pick up some straw and fly back directly to the nest.

Everything is wonderfully green now. It was unusually hot yesterday, in the eighties, and the asparagus has leapt up out of the ground, growing inches in twenty-four hours. I have to cut it every other day and the flavor is improving, now that it is growing faster. I've noticed that when asparagus or lettuce or carrots are just starting and are growing very slowly they are apt to be bitter. I suppose the juices are more concentrated.

This is a great year for the daffodils and narcissi. We have lots of them—single and double yellow, white, white with pink trumpets, yellow with orange trumpets. I like their names—Cheerfulness, Thalia, Mount Hood, Satin Pink, Silver Chimes and Actaea. But there is one name that doesn't quite fit—Mrs. R.O. Backhouse. I'm sure Mrs. Backhouse was pleased to have this lovely white daffodil with melon-pink trumpet named for her, but couldn't they have used her first name? The flower looks a lot like a Satin Pink but is much more mellifluous!

Patty phoned to say that Patrick hit a home run in his Little League game. It was only a short bunt but the pitcher fumbled and Patrick is such a fast runner that he made it to first base. Then another boy hit and Patrick tore around to second, third and home. His teammates hugged him, lifted him up in the air and one boy was so delighted that he gave him a nickel! Moment of glory!

Seeing a warbler is a mixed blessing. I try to notice all the field marks and look them up. So many warblers look alike, but rarely like the pictures in the bird book.

May 20. Went to the West Bolton Golf Club, three miles up our road. We joined the club so we can go up there for three-quarters of an hour and play four holes. When we used to pay each time, we felt obliged to play at least nine holes to get our money's worth. It's a beautiful spot, looking off to the mountains. Right now the wild apple trees, choke cherry, and wild cherry are in bloom, and tufts of skim-milk-colored bluets line the fairways. The golf is secondary.

May 31. Saw something beautiful today. Driving north from Bennington to Arlington on the new wide superhighway I saw a huge truck approaching from the north. At the same time I saw something small on my side of the road ahead of me. It was a mother duck followed by a comet tail of six tiny ducklings and they were headed straight across the road. I knew I had time to stop and I slowed down but I didn't have much faith in the truck. The duck sensed the danger, stopped, looked in my direction, turned and led her little string of puff balls back to safety on my side of the road. They didn't scatter or even break ranks. As I passed her, surrounded by the ducklings, I could see she was talking to them, no doubt pointing out the dangers and the rewards for obedience.

June 4. Someone, a rabbit?, has been getting into my small salad garden, chomping off the young lettuce and spinach plants, and worst of all, my early Lacy Lady peas! A garden tip on the tv suggested a remedy—of Epsom salts and one teaspoon Chlorox in one gallon of water. I dribbled it all around the edge of the fence. It seemed to work—no danger for two days—but this morning the peas and lettuce and even the radish tops were cropped off. Clara Manor told me I should spray it right on the plants. I'll try it and report later.

June 8. It didn't work but I think we've identified the culprit. George saw a big woodchuck sitting on the sunny stone doorstep of the barn near the salad garden. He shot it—a pretty good shot at two hundred yards—and killed it instantly. It was a female so we watched for young ones. The next day a nearly-grown chuck was in plain sight at the back of the old house. George shot and probably got it, but it dove under the old house. We tried to see it, looking with a flashlight and poking with a long pole. No luck. I am stonyhearted about woodchucks. They have plenty to eat out there besides my peas!

I check on our two bird families each day from a respectful distance. I can't see into the nests but I can stand under them and a little to one side so my view is of the bottom of the nest with mama's head and beak protruding on one side and her tail extending three or four inches on the other. The robin has been sitting on the nest for several days. My bird book says the incubation period is eleven to fourteen days. The blue jay started incubating a few days earlier. The incubation period for blue jays is twelve to seventeen days, so both families should be hatching any day soon.

June 6. And they have! This morning when I went down to feed the chickens I looked up in the pine tree just as a blue jay parent returned to the nest. Suddenly three or four heads reared up, stretching and jockeying for an advantageous position. I can't see their bodies so I don't know if they are newly hatched or beginning to feather out. The heads look pretty big, but then a blue jay is a big bird. Mama robin is still sitting tight on her eggs. Both nests are so high and so well-concealed that most of my progress notes are based on guesses.

Toad Hall

It isn't only a young man's fancy that lightly turns to thoughts of love in the spring. The lowly toad, *Bufo Terrestris*, berated or extolled in phrase and fable, has an irresistible urge to make his way from the woods where he has been hibernating, to the lake where he and his larger lady friend will spawn. Unfortuately the path of true love is seldom smooth and in Hambleden, England, thirty-five miles west of London, 3,000 toads have to cross the lethal Henley road to reach the site of their tryst. They travel only at night when there is no moon and hundreds of them are squashed by passing motorists. Since 1984 the Fauna and Flora Preservation Society has waged a crusade to save the toads by means of notices at more than two hundred migration sites and bumper stickers that say, "Help a toad across the road." But how many motorists are going to stop their cars and escort the toads to safety like the boy scout and the old lady? Shades of A.A. Milne and Kenneth Grahame! "There must be a better way," Pooh Bear grunted as Christopher Robin, holding him by one foot, bumped him unceremoniously down the stairs.

Now the good people of Hambleden have taken their cause a step farther and built England's first toad tunnel, ten inches in diameter, moist but ventilated to a toad's taste, which runs for twenty yards under the road.

The Wind in the Willows was written eighty years ago, but how delighted Kenneth Grahame would have been by this project! He wrote

The world has held great heroes,
    As history books have showed;
But never a name to go down to fame
    Compared to that of Toad!

The clever men at Oxford
    Know all that there is to be knowed
But they none of them know half as much
    As intelligent Mr. Toad.

Of course that was Toad's self-evaluation. It would have surpassed even Toad's dream of glory if he had known that his photograph and an article were to appear on the front page of the *New York Times* on March 14, 1987. I have no proof of a toad's intelligence. In fact, the people of Hambleden didn't rely on it heavily either and put fences of plastic sheeting along the edge of the woods to guide the toads towards amplexus rather than annihilation. You don't know what "amplexus" is? It's an eight-letter word for the over-worked three-letter word, "sex."

Shakespeare was familiar with, if not enamored of, toads. One of the most frequently quoted passages in *As You Like It* is

Sweet are the uses of adversity
Which like the toad, ugly and venemous,
Wears yet a precious jewel in his head;
And this our life, exempt from public haunt,
Finds tongues in trees, books in the running brooks,
Sermons in stones, and good in everything

I too find books in running brooks, sermons in stones, and believe there is good in almost everything. Even in toads. I have had some casual acquaintance with toads. There is an enormous one at the edge of our vegetable garden. He or his clone have been there for years. A toad can live as long as thirty-one years, so we are growing old together. He doesn't have a jewel in his head but his presence is precious to me because of his voracious appetite for all sorts of insects, snails, and other destructive creatures in the garden.

I like toads. Why do people use their name pejoratively? No one makes disparaging remarks about frogs except the occasional princess who prefers a suitor from her own species. Is there a color prejudice here? Is green more socially acceptable than brown? Or is it his bumpy skin that is distasteful to the general public? His warts are neither infectious nor transmissible.

What about the word "venomous?" A toad's only means of defense is an acrid, mildly irritating secretion from his skin which is not harmful. When Lord Skelmersdale, parliamentary undersecretary for environment, dedicated the toad tunnel in the name of the Queen and amphibians, he knelt in a muddy field, quoted Kipling, cut an appropriately small ribbon and said, "This is the first time I have actually held a toad and my sympathy goes very much to the toad." Then he suddenly passed the toad to someone else and wiped his hand on the grass.

"It wet his hand. They usually do when you hold them," explained Tom Langton, the society's toadmaster who, we presume, had had previous experience with toads. Langton expects that two hundred toads an hour will use this tunnel during the season of their migration. Another tunnel is nearby. A chain of tunnels is planned to ease the burden of the volunteers who have been helping the toads by the bucketful across the road. But what about the thousands of toads in other parts of England who don't have a convenient neighborhood tunnel? And then there are the mavericks, the independent ones who flatly refuse to be herded and rather enjoy the risks and excitement of toad roulette?

If you recall Toad in *The Wind in the Willows*, all decked out and resplendent in gaiters, goggles, enormous overcoat and gauntleted gloves, he always followed his own latest whim and turned a deaf ear to the admonitions of Mole, Rat or even the formidable Badger.

This makes me wonder about the student tunnel that passes beneath Williston Road on the campus of the University of Vermont. After a great hue and cry about the potential danger to students crossing this heavily-trafficked stretch of highway, the university built a subterranean passageway a good many years ago at a cost of $50,000. It would probably cost a quarter-of-a-million dollars now. But that was when people were just learning to sue anyone for injuries resulting from action taken at one's own risk. In theory, all students coming and going from the Redstone campus and the Living and Learning Center to their classes or library or the student center would pass through the tunnel provided for them. But do they? Some do and their parents and I appreciate their prudence. I don't enjoy dodging their classmates as they dart across between the cars, but it is better than squashing them like toads.

Just imagine the protest and uproar if THEY were herded by restraining walls and funneled into the tunnel. "Freedom of choice! If I am old enough to drive a car I am old enough to risk being hit by one."

Maybe there are sermons in stones and toads and tunnels. But in any case, bravo for Bufo! Long may he live!

How Sweet Is the Shepherd's Sweet Lot!

I don't care what the Whiffenpoof song says, don't waste your sympathy on the "poor little lambs who have lost our way."

We bought two nice little lambs from Mrs. Pollard in Underhill and resettled them in a fenced-in pasture which has been home for our sheep for quite a few years. They seemed happy enough, began eating the grass and after sniffing the grain suspiciously decided it was not only edible but gourmet fare. The first day we would glance out the window and admire how bucolic they looked, cropping the grass or relaxing on the stones near the barn.

So it was quite a surprise when a lady rang our doorbell and asked if we knew that our two lambs were about a quarter of a mile up the road. Into our boots and off we went, but of course when we trotted after them they just trotted faster on their agile little tip-hooves. We tried to circle ahead of them and turn them back. George was able to catch one because it was trying to force its way through the fence of another pasture. I assumed that when the captured lamb baa-ed its friend would follow after, like Mary's little lamb. But the lamb George was carrying didn't baa and carrying a struggling lamb bears no resemblance to carrying a child of the same weight. The child hangs on but a lamb misleads you by being passive and then suddenly exploding into a spasm of kicking.

So I galloped back home for the truck, and George and the struggling lamb got in the back in plain view of the one still playing hard-to-get in the road. Finally the lady and I circled and shooed and maneuvered it back to our driveway and into the pasture.

We walked the fence and put extra fencing, so-called sheep fencing, where we suspected they had pushed through, and smugly returned to the house.

Not two hours later they were out on the road again, heading east with increased determination. If you could credit sheep with any homing instincts you might think they were trying to get back to the Pollard farm. But indicative of the usefulness of a sheep's brain they were headed in the wrong direction. I could hear a car approaching at high speed so when it appeared around the corner I waved it down to a slower speed, pointing to the unconcerned lambs. The nice young man in the red car pulled to the side of the road, got out, and summing up my predicament, circled them slowly. After various feints and plunges we returned them once more to the pasture.

Now I know a sheep is an animal of very little brain, but I am beginning to wonder about Wolfs. Wouldn't you think after two escapes I would give some thought to maximum security? Wrong. They were out again within an hour. I still thought I could fortify what I thought was the escape hatch, but as Clarence Manor pointed out, if a sheep can get his head through a hole, the rest of him follows after.

This time with the help of a man who stopped his truck we once again put them behind what I hoped was a barricade braced by a couple of wooden doors and fence posts. They looked peaceful as well as very tired so I set off for Essex Junction.

When I returned two hours later I noticed several people and two cars about a quarter of a mile west of our house but thought nothing of it. No sooner was I in the house than Nancy Smith came to the door and said that she and her son Michael and a friend were the people down the road and they were trying to keep our sheep contained in a bushy spot. When Nancy had passed our house earlier she had seen the sheep loose, stopped at our house, found no one at home, drove back to her house, got Michael, their truck and some rope, and was hoping to get the lambs in their truck and take them to their farm.

So once again I set off in our truck back down the road to where the two sheep, the Smiths and their friend were eyeing each other suspiciously. George came home at that point and four large people were able to catch two small sheep and put them in the back of our truck. Michael and George each straddled a lamb placed in a sitting position, because for some reason known only to sheep they are somewhat immobilized in that undignified squat.

Now we may be slow learners but eventually the light bulb turned on over our heads. This time the sheep were carried into the barn, dumped unceremoniously into the empty pig pen and boarded up halfway to the ceiling.

The sheep had been quite a bargain which had warmed the cockles of my Yankee heart, briefly. The next day we had to pay $50 for stronger fencing and build them a new playpen within their former pasture. When Blake wrote, "How sweet is the shepherd's sweet lot!" he should have turned it from a statement into a question.

And from now on I'm going to change the spelling of the refrain after the last line of the Whiffenpoof song.

"God have mercy on such as we."

Bah! Bah! Bah!

Le Plus Ça Change, Le Plus C'est la Même Chose

Thirty-five years ago, when Patty and Debbie were little, one of their kittens was run over. I was afraid they would be upset by this small tragedy, but after the first moments of disbelief they threw themselves into funeral plans with gusto. It took them an hour to dig a grave through the thick sod under the apple trees. A shoe box was found, daisies and buttercups were clutched in small fists and Patty, who could print, made a headstone of sorts out of a piece of cardboard. The kitten was accorded military honors in the form of a three cap-pistol salute. The cap-pistol belonged to Debbie so she insisted on firing the weapon, but because she hated the noise she commissioned Patty to stand behind her and put her fingers in Debbie's ears.

In the winter of 1986, when Patty's boys were seven and nine, their pet hamster breathed his last. The boys were saddened briefly. Peter asked, "Why can't you turn back into alive again?" But after accepting the finality of Squeaky's demise, they got busy with a funeral. The grave site was in their yard. Patrick gave the eulogy, "Here lies Squeaky, a true friend. We will never forget you." And the earth continued on its appointed rounds.

In a world that changes so rapidly it is comforting to a grandmother to find that things rather than people change. I helped one day at four-year-old Morgan's nursery school. It had been forty-one years since I had taught nursery school in Greenwich Village and Sarah Lawrence College. Those were the war years. We had no car, no tv, no one had visited the moon or explored outer space. But what the children were doing was exactly the same in 1986 as it had been in the '40s.

It is mind boggling to think of all the words a small child has to learn. And in Patrick and Peter's case, not only in English but in Finnish, Swedish and Danish as well. Peter said his teacher wasn't in school because he had "jewelry duty." He told his mother that his art teacher had forehead all the way over his head except around his ears and in back. Patrick asked me if I knew he was "precocious" in a tone that implied it was a communicable disease. Morgan called me "Blabby" until he was three. I had no idea why, although other irreverent members of the family have made snide remarks by way of explanation. When Patrick was four, he went to Willy Cochran's art class. He was unfamiliar with the word "teacher" and called Willy his "art mama."

Being a grandmother is humbling as well as gratifying. When we visited the grandchildren in Denmark, Patrick and I were playing a game where you find hidden objects within a picture. He was much quicker at finding them than I. When

I complimented him on his observation he said, "Your eyes are too old. They don't get enough exercise. But if you do this every day you'll make the muscles in your eyes younger."

Any suggestions for making the muscles in my memory younger?

With all the languages and dialects in the world, thousands of them, it is a wonder that we can communicate at all. I admire the ability of Tage Strom, my son-in-law, to speak at least 9 languages fluently when sometimes George and I can completely misunderstand each other in English. If you have tried to read the directions that come with an appliance made in Japan you know that a literal translation often is quite different from common usage of the same words.

My favorite example is in front of a combined cafe and gas station in Richmond, Vermont. The sign reads "Eat here and get gas."

When Patty was tutoring Finnish people in English, one pupil came in somewhat after the appointed hour and gasped, "I am so sorry to be retarded."

When my parents went to China eighty years ago they were fascinated by some of the signs on city stores meant to lure the English-speaking visitors. One tailor shop announced, "Ladies have their fits upstairs, Gents have their fits on the street."

But when their train stopped in small towns and local vendors were hawking their wares, fruits and hard-boiled eggs, to the passengers, my father, who was an accomplished mimic, confounded the poor hard-boiled-egg vendor by picking up an egg, putting it to his ear and making the peeping sound of a chick. Language wasn't needed. The poor egg salesman was surrounded by a laughing crowd.

In some villages the Chinese women had never seen a white woman and my mother's skirts to the ground and huge veiled hat drew curious stares. The bolder ones touched her clothes tentatively and shook their heads disapprovingly at her wide hazel eyes, long (to them) pointed nose and high-buttoned shoes. But when she approached a young mother with a baby, smiled, patted its head and blew it a kiss, the Chinese mother didn't need any words to understand her admiration.

Maybe we talk too much and say too little.

And a Little Child
Shall Weed Them

Don't count on it! What a little child pulls up in your garden is a potato plant "to see if it has made any potatoes on the bottom yet."

My own children now have small children of their own to "help" in the garden. Serves them right! When Debbie was two or three I always took her to the garden with me, not so much to interest her in horticulture as to keep her from getting into trouble alone in the house. If I yelped, "Don't step on the tomatoes," she didn't step on them, she sat on them. She pulled up the toothpick-size carrots for her dolls and gathered pea blossoms to add to her fistful of dandelions. She loved to dig but had a very cavalier attitude about where. I finally gave up trying to garden except when she was asleep or, preferably, visiting a friend.

When they got old enough to know parsley from purslane our daughters couldn't be bribed to help. Patty would pull a few weeds, ask if it had been fifteen minutes yet at two-minute intervals and then decide she had heard the telephone ring. Whether it was really ringing or merely a figment of her wishful thinking, she rarely returned to the garden.

They had lots of complaints. Worms were too wiggly. The sun was too hot or the wind too cold. There was a stone in their shoes or a bee was being too friendly. In fact the biggest pests in the garden were two small girls who would rather be somewhere else and soon were.

Guess who are avid gardeners now? The same. They both raise flowers and vegetables with a little more emphasis on flowers. I grow flowers and vegetables too, with a lot more success with vegetables. According to my husband I only care about plants that I can eat. He's partly right, 'though the first flowers of spring, snowdrops and crocuses, do a lot for my winter-weary spirits. Both daughters have had greenhouses. Patty's was in Denmark and Debbie's in South Burlington, Vermont. Where did I go right? Probably they sensed that I was having a good time in the garden and when they had one they could call their own, so did they.

Debbie's Morgan, the youngest of our three beautiful and exceptional grandsons, liked to lead me around their garden when he was four, admiring the flowers and warning me not to pick tiny green tomatoes or green strawberries, "only wed ones." He also pulled up a tiny bean plant to show me the bean "that grew on the bottom!" I rushed to save the bean crop before he decided that that was the way you picked beans. When he was three and "helping", Debbie stuck white markers at the end of her raised bed rows telling what was planted in each row. As she was finishing up along came

Morgan proudly showing her the fistful of markers that he had removed from the rows to "help".

Patty's boys at ages seven and nine were quite knowledgeable, but allergic to sustained effort in the garden. Peter would pull up a carrot and eat it, dirt and all. The ring around his mouth that used to bear the purple stain of grape juice became brown from mother earth. Patrick thought the only vegetable worth eating was a potato, but he was willing to nibble tentatively on dill (his Scandinavian heritage) or broccoli with cheese sauce. Both boys are in accord with President Reagan in believing not only that ketchup is a vegetable but the best one. They did help me dig potatoes last summer and with fewer impaled potatoes than when George forks them up, but weeding is still low on their preferred activities list. In fact it is right down there with going back to school in the fall and visiting people who have no kids with Transformers.

The pre-teen girl may take an interest in a garden plot that is strictly her own, preferably for commercial purposes, like selling Indian corn to the local florist. But when boys begin to look better than beans, the green pigment in her thumbs fades like the autumn leaves. It will come back, maybe not for another ten years, but it is fun when your adult children become consultants and colleagues over the garden fence.

Much of what I have learned about gardening has been through trial and error, mostly error. Books are fine for midwinter reading and occasional reference for the care and feeding of something exotic, but the only way you really learn how to is by learning how not to.

When we planted our first garden thirty-six years ago my ignorance was deeper than abysmal. I had grown up in the

41

suburbs where my father sometimes had a small garden and my mother expected her perennials to look after themselves. Neither one enlisted my help, probably with good reason. And if any pearls of horticultural wisdom were cast in my direction they never rolled into my range of teen-age interests.

So when we bought a small hillside farm in northern Vermont to balance our winter city life by summer country life, a garden was my first priority. I went to Bloomingdale's and bought a seed packet of everything that looked familiar. To get a head start I started seeds in flats several weeks before we left for Vermont. Do you think I started tomato and pepper seeds and perhaps some flowers? Wrong. I started corn, beans and lettuce. The hoots of derision from friends whose thumbs were greener than mine made me keep this a guilty secret until this year when I read an article about a man who *always* starts his corn indoors. My transplants did grow too even after their exhaust-filled ride in the trunk of our car, 325 miles from Manhattan to Jericho Center.

There must be a guardian angel for novice gardeners. We arranged for a neighbor to plow and harrow a small piece of our meadow. He actually did it on the date specified which we didn't know was unique in the local mores of "helping out." Then we came up and planted it one Saturday in mid-May. The day was sunny and there were no subsequent frosts that year!

After the corn transplants my next goof was planting a whole packet of parsley seeds. Packets contained more in those days. We had a hedge of parsley when it finally came up, enough to garnish every entree on the eastern seaboard. I also planted pumpkins with jack-o-lanterns in mind. The seed I bought was Connecticut Field and it was apparent by mid-August that The Great Pumpkin and his whole family had arrived in our garden. A farmer neighbor jokingly suggested that I take them to the Champlain Valley Fair. I did and my guardian angel pinned a blue ribbon on our outsize cucurbits. Heady stuff for a beginner and I was hooked by the hoe forever.

But the bit of my gardening which caused the most snickering in Jericho Center was the way I planted the seed potatoes. I had been told to plant them in the dark of the moon. It was dark all right as I crept along the row with a flashlight, tucking in each piece at 10:00 P.M.! You might expect that after that first year I would do everything right and our garden would be the envy of the village. You would be wrong. Each year we have some successes and some failures. My first encounter with tomato hornworms nearly ended my gardening career but I've never seen one since. We rarely have corn earworms or blossom-end rot. But we've had more than our share of cucumber beetles, broccoli that was enjoyed by woodchucks rather than Wolfs and scrofulous potatoes.

We learn slowly. We solve one problem and are confronted by a new one. This year George built me a tepee for the pole beans and now they are so far beyond my reach that I have to play "Jack and the Beanstalk."

Oh well! It all began in a garden long, long ago and with a little luck I hope that's where it will end for me. They can just dig a hole right where I drop with my garden boots on. There's no place I'd rather spend eternity.

Houdini, Where Are You
When I Need You?

How can someone tamper with a bottle of Tylenol capsules or a package of Lipton's Cup-a-Soup and replace it, leaving no trace of the crime when, as a legal consumer, I have to pry, poke and blast my way into many containers?

I'm not talking about pill bottles now. I've already had my say on that subject in the past and I'm glad that some manufacturers now print "package not child resistant" on their product. I can hardly take credit for that but obviously I was not the only one left on the outside of simple medications.

One of my current frustrations is trying to get the little white plastic strip off the frozen orange juice cans. Sometimes it pulls right off and gives me a head start on the good day everyone tells me to have. But far too often, after the first yank and broken fingernail, the white strip turns out to be imbedded in the edge of the can and refuses to budge. The only recourse is cutting the lid off with a conventional can opener. So much for convenient packaging.

Another hurdle in the obstacle race of domesticity is prying out the little metal circle that is fastened inside the lid of a maple syrup can. You unscrew the cap only to face this new barrier which can't be removed except by jamming a hole in it with a sharp object and prying it up. Maple syrup isn't perishable enough to require double seals.

I'm sure that the manufacturers never use the products they package. If some kind friend sends you citrus fruit from Florida, it arrives in a box hermetically sealed with two-inch brass staples that require pliers and the strength of Arnold S. to remove. Glued-down cardboard isn't much easier. After prying one corner you have to put one foot on the box and yank with all your might. A small piece rips off in your hand and you collapse on the floor.

If the box has not been secured with staples or glue it may have been taped with Permacel, that innocent-looking sealing tape that looks like opaque Scotch tape but actually conceals myriad strands of the world's strongest thread. It can't be torn. It has to be loosened and cut.

I like crisp crackers and if I lived in a humid climate I might bless Messrs. Keebler and Sunshine, but the current boxes of Saltines remind me of those toys shaped like nested eggs where the big egg contains a slightly smaller one of a different color and so on until you finally come on one the size of a hummingbird's egg. Inside the cardboard cracker box is a plastic bag. Inside the plastic bag are four more plastic envelopes that are tightly sealed. They can only be ripped open with two hands and deleted expletives.

While I'm complaining about packaging materials, what do you do with all those little styrofoam shells that are stuffed around anything fragile? For a while I saved them in a plastic bag thinking I might use them when I needed to mail some delicate object. But it is becoming clear that I don't mail delicate objects very often. I am a consumer rather than a distributor. After I had two plastic bags and a drawer full

45

of those feather-like amoebae it became obvious that rather than fill our entire house with styrofoam shells I'd better donate them to the local sanitary landfill (dump). I doubt if they are biodegradable. Future archaeologists will believe our diet included little more than cold cereal and whatever mollusks lived in styrofoam sea shells. But now I've found a use for them. Dick Raymond, the garden expert, says they are just the thing for drainage in the bottom of flower pots instead of small pebbles which are hard to find under two feet of snow, or broken bits of flowerpots which most of us don't hoard.

I can understand why cash should not be sent through the mail but why does my monthly bank statement have to come in an envelope that is glued down with an adhesive so strong that I have to hold the envelope in one hand and pull as hard as I can with the other hand to release the contents? Surely my cancelled checks can't be top secret. Simple stickum would suffice.

It is possible for your everyday thief to slide a credit card past a spring lock and enter your house, which happened to us in New York City and in Kansas. We learn slowly but we did install deadbolts in Kansas. If your robber is more athletically inclined, he can kick in the door, ripping off the door frame as one did to us in Jericho. That was more expensive. The insurance company paid for the stolen silver, but it cost more than the insurance money for a new door frame and the installation of a security system.

If these forced entries are not only possible but common, why should it be harder for me to open a package addressed to me that contains a product that I have ordered and paid for?

Gardens: Pray as You Sow Plan

What is so rare as a day in June when you find your garden unblemished and unscathed, just the way it looked the day before? I'm not talking about big game. Of course deer can be a real problem. Our woods are full of deer, except during the hunting season, but they have mercifully taken to the hills in June. However, the woodchucks and the raccoons are always with us. Fortunately the raccoons leave our garden alone until the corn season. We use an electric wire strung a few inches above the fence for those few weeks. It's an expense and a bit of a nuisance. In fact it can be quite a shock if you touch it by mistake, but it is nothing compared to the shock of finding most of your corn ears half-eaten and strewn around the corn patch. Before we tried electric shock therapy (the shock is for the raccoons, the therapy is for the Wolfs) we had tried all the old wives' and husbands' suggestions and I am here to tell you that red pepper, pumpkin-vine prickles, human-hair clippings, dried blood and radios only whet a raccoon's appetite.

In June it is rabbits and woodchucks that want to beat us to the gnaw. A woodchuck can find a weak spot in the fence where he can shove his fat self under or dig out a stage door for his evening performance. A Havahart big trap just outside the fence sometimes works but I must admit we rarely have a heart. With my blessing and my fingers in my ears George has been known to shoot the 'chuck and recycle him in the garden. After all, he could thrive just as well on the clover and grasses that we don't relish. A woodchuck has neither the grace of a deer, the cleverness of a raccoon or the charm of a baby rabbit. They aren't even useful on Groundhog Day in Vermont because we always have more than six weeks of additional winter whether he sees his shadow or not.

But even if nothing furry has visited your garden overnight, June is when I find the first Colorado potato beetle. I have no qualms about picking off the full-grown ones and stamping on them. They are not repulsive but the immature ones, the larvae, are soft and red and cling to your fingers. I prefer to knock them into a can. At the same time striped cucumber beetles have discovered the squash and those little black leaf hoppers are trying to make lace out of the cucurbit leaves and tomato vines. I am lazy enough to rely on rotenone rather than brewing up one of thoses garlic teas that the organic gardeners favor. But that doesn't do anything to discourage those little white moths that are hunting through the broccoli plants to find a good spot for egg laying. It helps later when their progeny, the green cabbage worms appear. I marvel at the wormless broccoli in the supermarket, but I don't dare ask what insecticide they use.

What does make June days rare is that there is something new, besides beasts and bugs, in your garden every day. The peas have blossomed and so have the potatoes. The lettuce and spinach are at their tender best and the radishes young and tasty. A huge orange squash blossom has unfolded like an upturned parasol and there is a fat bee murmuring at its heart. We eat asparagus every day in June—in soup, hot, cold, under Hollandaise or over toast. On a warm day the growth of an asparagus spear is clearly visible. If you haven't time to squat down and watch it grow you can stick a ruler in the ground and see where the tip is at 4:00 P.M. compared to where it was after breakfast.

It's easy to forget the unwanted fauna when the sun is warm on your back, the breeze gentle, the weeds come up root and all without giving you an argument and a robin is helping herself to a bit of mud for her nest in the apple tree.

Reunion

When I was teaching nursery school at Sarah Lawrence College, the school medical advisor was a young pediatrician destined for wider recognition. His name was Benjamin Spock. At a meeting of the parents he said, "It's too bad you can't start parenting with a second child because you are much more sensible with second sight." The same is true with the initial shock of a fiftieth college reunion. You should throw away that first half hour when you wonder *who* all those *old* people are. By the second half hour you find that they are the same friends you knew fifty years ago.

I remember the first reunion. Being the youngest reunion class we were bedded down on wall-to-wall cots in the ancient gym. We talked most of the night and the topics were jobs, graduate school, marriage and a class baby who at the time of our fiftieth is forty-nine years old.

At our twenty-fifth reunion it was our kids trying to get

in or out of college, our aging parents, and our ectomies—
hyster- and mast-.

Now with the fiftieth it is retirement life-styles, cruises to
Alaska, the Norwegian fjords, the Greek islands, and our
exceptional grandchildren. A woman's life can be read in
the contents of her pocketbook. Now it contains pictures
of the grandchildren, hypertensive medication and *AARP*
cards. We tell each other, "You haven't changed," and perhaps
inside we haven't, but the world has.

This was pointed out by Nardi Reeder Campion a few years
ago at her forty-fifth Wellesley reunion. She said, "We were
before tv, before polio shots and Frisbees. Before nylon, tv
dinners, Xerox, Kinsey, radar, fluorescent lights, credit cards,
and ballpoint pens. A chip meant a piece of wood. Before
women could vote in France. Before La Guardia and Logan
airports, Israel and the UN. Before India, Pakistan, Indonesia,
the Philippines and Iceland were independent countries.
Before Alaska and Hawaii became states. Before dripdry and
pantyhose. Before dishwashers and electric blankets. We were
before Best's and Peck and Peck folded. American schools
were not desegregated. A college year cost $1,000–$500 for
room and board, $500 for tuition. And, God help us all,
before nuclear fission."

I'd like to add a few of my own. We were before women
could climb the corporate ladder without pain. Hardware
was hammer and nails. Before students had keys to the
dorms. Before men wore long hair and earrings. If you had
a permanent wave you endured being attached to a hot,
heavy machine that cooked your hair to a frizz.

Back to Nardi, "There were five-and-ten-cent stores which
sold things for five and ten cents. For just one nickel you
could ride the subway or the ferry, make a 'phone call, mail

two letters and a postcard. You could buy a new Chevy coupe for $659 but who could afford that in 1936? Too bad. Gas was eleven cents a gallon. Cigarettes were in fashion, grass was mowed and coke was to drink."

Now just think of what we *did* have in 1936 at Mt. Holyoke. We had big sisters and dorm rooms that were never locked. We had Mountain Day – a surprise in October when the chapel bell rang continuously to tell us that classes would be cancelled and we should take to the hills to enjoy the autumn foliage at its peak. We had the Junior Prom and Saturday night dances where we were the stag line. We had daily chapel and required courses in speech, freshman English, and hygiene, where it was suggested that our marriages would be successful if we put the cap back on the toothpaste after using it. No wonder so many of our marriages have lasted! We had hats and white gloves and maids who shoved a little dust around the halls. We had cries of "Junior Lunch 5¢" in Post Office corridor and spit cards at Christmas. This was an ugly name for a friendly custom of putting tiny notes adorned with a Christmas seal into the mailboxes of your friends and faculty members. We had Mr. Buss's taxi which could take ten girls to the movies. We had Peg Moore Hartman as May Queen and Flops Dunbar Robertson winning the Sarah Streeter cup with Sarah Streeter's daughter, Jane Lester, a member of our class.

The only drugs we knew were at Glessie's drugstore and they were aspirin and Midol. We had those awful centrally-controlled showers after gym which made you feel that all that was lacking was a cattle prod. And how about those nude posture pictures where the details of your anatomy were dictated to a blessedly uninterested assistant! We had role models and heroes, concerts and movies starring Katherine

Hepburn or Ronald Coleman. We had Margaret Sanger speak to us about birth control—in 1936! Gertrude Stein talked to us while Alice B. Toklas sat in the front row knitting. We had Mr. Felici in the village to repair our shoes even though a pair of saddle shoes only cost $4.95. We had Mr. Warbeke striding across campus in his enormous opera cape and the rumor that his brain was to be given to Harvard at his demise. We admired the dignity of Miss Wooley and her efforts for world peace and understanding, and we scuttled meekly when she phoned South Rocky Hall to say that the young ladies who were sunning in bathing suits on the sunparlor roof should go indoors *immediately!*

We had the flood of 1936 when men from the village and nearby farms drove us over the back roads to the flooded Springfield railroad station where we scrambled up ramps to the second floor to catch our trains for New York or Boston. We could have a car on campus the second semester of our senior year only if we had a B average. No male was allowed above the first floor. We mailed our laundry home in cardboard containers and it came back with the hometown newspaper and brownies or in Ginnie Taylor Potsubay's case, a wonderful Scandinavian smorgasbord—ah, the Limpa, the herring and liver pate, which started me on a lifelong addiction to Scandinavian food. We had all the big bands—Tommy Dorsey, Glen Gray, Guy Lombardo—songs like "Night and Day" and "Body and Soul." Dancing was a contact sport rather than a spastic affliction. It was romantic and so were we.

What we didn't have was fear of the atom bomb, drug abuse, rampant mugging and carcinogenic food. If it was, we didn't know it. Closets were for clothes. We had never heard of AIDS. Gay meant "Blithe Spirit." Playboy was the hero of Synge's drama. We didn't take a year off to find ourselves. We didn't know we were lost.

How little we knew! How much to discover! We didn't know that labor pains may not be the most painful part of having children and that once you are a parent, their problems are with you for life. In spite of dating we were vastly ignorant about some fundamental differences between men and women. I don't mean anatomically. Miss Morgan's Baby Zoology lectures gave us facts. I mean we didn't know that a man would rather wander through a city for an hour than ask directions, and that anything lost in your household has been hidden by you, not mislaid by him. We didn't know that a man can tie a microscopic trout fly but cannot thread a needle. Women like to discard clothes. A trip to the Salvation Army makes her feel shriven. Men cling to them like sniffy blankets. But men are splendid about remembering what is tax-exempt or the internal workings of the combustion engine.

We have learned that the empty nest can be a cozy spot. We can get along just fine now without Girl Scouts, Little League, rock and roll, and the confusion and pendulum swings of teenagers. Our children have become our friends and they treat us kindly and almost solicitously.

What we did have fifty years ago was hope, enthusiasm and a sure belief that we would improve the world. We were lucky and the fact that so many of us came to this reunion shows that we had endurance. We used to be slightly embarrassed to be called Mt. Holyoke Types or worse yet, greasy grinds. Now we are proud of it and proud of ourselves, proud of our college and, when we consider the alternative, proud of being three-score-and-ten-plus years old.

It All Came Out in the Wash

People bemoan the lack of neighborliness these days. It is blamed on the fact that in many cases both parents work outside the home, or that families move more often than formerly, or that crime has made everyone suspicious of unfamiliar faces.

But I know why we know so little about our neighbors. It is because laundry no longer is hung outdoors to dry. Here in Vermont the country wife still may hang her laundry on the front porch, but in the cities and suburbs only your drier knows for sure the contents of your laundry hamper.

When I was growing up you could see your neighbor's clothesline from your kitchen window, and you didn't have to be Sherlock Holmes to tell what each family was up to.

When diapers were supplanted by small underpants you knew that at last Billy Jones was toilet trained. When there were more sheets than usual on the line, the Robinsons had been having overnight guests. Beach towels and tennis clothes proclaimed that the Smiths had been on vacation. When sport shirts and wash pants replaced white dress shirts on the clothesline it meant that Mr. Walker had lost his job. In fact, Mr. Walker was out there setting up the rotating umbrella type of clothespost that was folded up and stored in the cellar when not in use. A big Irish-linen tablecloth and napkins meant a dinner party, and a washing hung out as late as 11 A.M. meant that Mrs. Smith had gone back to sleep after Mr. Smith had left for the 8:10 A.M. commuter train.

In some neighborhoods laundry was hung out at the same time every Monday morning, and Mrs. Jones and Mrs. Smith or their laundresses paused to chat over the hedge. Recipes and the children's progress in school were exchanged. They noticed that the Robinson boy was home on leave from the Navy because bell-bottom trousers were flapping on the family's line. That reminded Mrs. Jones that the Robinson boy might like to meet her niece from Ann Arbor who was here for the week, and when she found out that Mrs. Smith couldn't get to the store because Jimmy had chicken pox she offered to sit with him while Mrs. Smith went shopping. It was like the symbiosis that some plants and wildlife share—milkweed and monarch butterflies, for instance. They needed each other and shared more than a street address.

When I was a child I knew everyone on the block and had been in and out of all of the houses. When we were married and lived at 1303 York Avenue in New York City we knew many of the other tenants because we had a mutual

56

bond in New York Hospital where some members of each household worked. But when we moved to a fancier apartment I never knew or even saw the people living in the apartments on the same floor. To borrow a cup of sugar would have been a shocking infringement on their privacy. Perhaps down in the laundry room in the basement formal greetings might be exchanged but nothing more.

One of the things I like about living in the country is that we still help each other out of a ditch or an illness. There are many new people on our road whom I don't know and perhaps won't because most of the young couples are both working and we no longer have children of school age. But the old-timers, in residence as well as in age, who are not gainfully employed outside of the home still live symbiotically with our neighbors.

Morris Gittleson, in his eighties and living alone since his wife died, now has a live-in housekeeper but he hasn't been well enough to drive and she doesn't have a license. So the obvious solution, monitored by one of the neighbors, is that four of us each have a week when we take Anna to the grocery store.

I don't mean to imply that electric driers have sucked out neighborliness along with the rinse water, but so much of our lives that used to be in full view is now hidden. Even in the country mothers are away from home at their jobs, children go from school to a sitter or organized activities rather than walking home and playing in their neighborhoods. We always walked and took an active interest in everything that was happening along the route. Now the children are dropped off by the school bus in front of their own or the sitter's house. The neighbor's cow or a disabled car is just a passing blur and not a reason for immediate involvement. But the enthusiasm of the volunteer fire department and the local rescue squads show that no matter where your laundry dries, people still want to help out in times of trouble.

Is There Life after Radicchio and Sushi?

It isn't only oil or small cars that we have imported from the Middle East and Japan. Now it is couscous and sashimi. One of the reasons for a trip to France used to be to enjoy the French cuisine, and Scandinavian smorgasbords ranked right up there with fjords and saunas.

I grew up with a pasta acquaintance limited to Franco-American spaghetti and macaroni and cheese. But now a menu reads like a travel brochure and a chapter from Euell Gibbons.

The only trouble with international cuisine is that it is as subject to fashion whims as haute couture. Beef Wellington no longer is served at state dinners. Quiche and crepes are not as high on the culinary totem pole as they used to be. Sashimi and sushi are chic. Tofu has become a naturalized staple along with yoghurt, but yoghurt's old-fashioned cousin, junket, is never suggested, even for children.

Pasta is in and gourmets bestow their favor and pesto on fusilli, manicotti and fettucini garnished with Italian, not curly, parsley.

Mushrooms have gone wild. Cepes, morels and shiitake are more socially acceptable than the domesticated white buttons from eastern Pennsylvania. Do you remember when salads, like Gaul, were divided in three parts? It was either potato, Waldorf or a slice of pineapple on iceberg lettuce supporting a cube of cream cheese.

No more! If you have a taste for fruit salad you must include kiwi, star fruit or mango. *In* greens are pak choy, radicchio, ragula or anything wild that isn't proven toxic. When I was a child in New Jersey it was only the Italian women who would dig up dandelion greens from our lawns and parks. Now dandelion greens are washed and in plastic at the supermarket produce area along with watercress and Belgian endive.

Nouvelle cuisine has been assimilated but it is no longer a topic of conversation. Regional cooking is booming even though, ironically enough, it is done in restaurants far from the region, rather than in the home. Cajun jambalayas and gumbos are as much at home in New York as on the bayou, although by the time you read this they may have returned to the south.

What has happened to meat and potatoes? They are still with us but you must leave the skins on the potatoes and be sure to marinate the meat. Who would dare to serve pot roast and mashed potatoes to anyone but the immediate family? I would but I'm not worried about being au courant.

I applaud the demise of mixed peas and carrots next to

a patty shell filled with creamed chicken, followed by striped vanilla, chocolate and strawberry ice cream that were required birthday party fare in my childhood, but I'm afraid we are being manipulated all over again. Not everyone prefers raw squid and seaweed to a tuna-fish sandwich.

And poi and polenta aren't high on my list of favorites.

Brown rice and brown bread taste better and do more for you than the white kinds of both, but we've spent 200 years going from wood stoves to oil burners and now we're back to lugging logs and grinding our own wheat.

And now the all-American backyard barbeque is being done up in a French twist. Charcoal and gas never aspired to being conversation pieces but what you burn is becoming as important as what you grill. For some time it has been socially acceptable to argue the merits of mesquite if you winter in the southwest, alder wood if you were raised near Seattle or apple and hickory anywhere in the east. But now California, always trendy, whets its appetite with vintage-dated grapevine cuttings from France as fuel for the grill.

In a recent issue of *Food and Wine* magazine an article on grilling by Alan Richman says that Vernon Rollins, co-chef and co-owner of the New Boonville Hotel in Boonville, California, reports that his customers not only can tell the difference between hardwoods, they can also tell the difference between food cooked over Riesling vine cuttings and food cooked over Gewurtztraminer vine cuttings. He says that Chardonnay adds the strongest flavor, Riesling the most delicate. Well, Californians believe in health cults and Ronald Reagan too.

Fashions in food and its preparation change as often as

fads in clothing. Sometimes they last more than a season and sometimes they are only affectations that neither taste good nor look well on most of us.

"Chaçun a son goût" and my "goût" is for an occasional foreign adventure but with the reassurance that I can return to the familiar landscape in food as well as geography.

The Scent of Summer

On the first morning after Debbie, Steve, and Morgan had moved from South Burlington to the country, five-year-old Morgan went out on the long deck and shouted, "Smell the nature!" What was he smelling on June 16? Was it new-mown hay, field flowers or the sun on the wooden deck?

The smells of summer evoke memories that reach far back into our childhoods. Even though our house is surrounded by pine trees, when the sun warms our pines what I remember is the tall pine grove along the Kennebec River in Hinckley, Maine where I spent several childhood summers. And I can recall the smell of wet, woolen bathing suits and rubber bathing caps, smells that are now as obsolete as dinosaurs.

Official summer began with the Fourth of July and that meant the smell of punk and fireworks and watermelon along with the crepe paper that we wove in and out of the spokes of our bicycles.

If you were blindfolded and suddenly had to tell the season

63

by relying only on your sense of smell, where would spring end and summer begin? Here in Vermont apple blossoms mean spring and come in late May just before Memorial Day when lilacs perfume the dooryard of every farm. On Cape Cod, the first wild roses mean the beginning of summer, and everywhere in New England when you opened up the summer camp or cottage you were greeted by an aromatic melange of wicker furniture, musty mattresses, unfinished wood, kerosene and wood smoke that meant the whole beautiful summer stretched ahead into infinity. At the shore there is always what my mother-in-law called "the smell of salt," which really had less to do with salt than the evaporation from the wet tidal flats and the myriad organisms exposed to the sun. In Maine the summer is fragrant with bay and balsam and the unmistakable fishy smell of the bait they put in the lobster traps. There is the milder smell of new tennis balls when you open the vacuum can and the ropey smell of the tennis net when you gather it up in your arms to carry it out to the court.

Now in Vermont full summer begins with the heavy sweet scent of milkweed. I don't welcome its plants in the garden. You can pull up the shoots easily but the root goes on with an underground life of its own, sending up shoots all over the place. In spite of Euell Gibbons and Scott Nearing, I'd rather eat our asparagus or fiddleheads than the young shoots of milkweed which poke up at the same time. I don't trust anything that exudes white juice except a cow. But the bees and I love the smell of the mauve-rose blossoms.

The scent of tomato vines is another evocative summer smell. I spend a lot of time pinching out the suckers between the branches of the indeterminate tomatoes and my fingers

64

pick up that distinctive tomato smell. It stays with me until I wash my hands and then it dissolves into aromatic yellow suds.

One of the most comforting summer smells is that of laundry dried in the sun. They tell me the sun and wind are harder on fibers than our mechanical driers but I'll trade in the longer linen life for the pleasure of sniffing sun-dried sheets and towels.

To anyone with a boat the smell of paint, tar and canvas means summer. And there are city smells of summer—hot street pavement that squishes underfoot, and food carts at every corner with an international assortment of Mid-Eastern and Mediterranean specialities such as knishes, shish kebobs, pita bread sandwiches and gnocchi.

Around the fourth of July we pick our own strawberries at a nearby berry farm. A good part of the pleasure in this early summer expedition comes from the wonderful fragrance of the ripe berries. As you creep along on the straw-covered aisles, sometimes on your knees, occasionally squashing a berry and staining your fingers with the juice of an over-ripe berry, the sun is warm on your back and the scent of the moist earth and straw blends with the fragrance of the strawberries.

It is a fragrance that evokes memories of long ago strawberry socials on the church lawn, homemade strawberry ice cream that you cranked endlessly on the back porch so that you could lick the ambrosia-covered dasher, or a strawberry sundae in the cool, dark vanilla-scented atmosphere of an old-fashioned ice cream parlor, with its small marble-topped tables and the wire-backed chairs that made round prints on your damp shoulders.

Barefoot

Shoe the old horsie
Shoe the old mare
But let the little coltie's
Feet go bare.
　　　　　　　　　—Old nursery rhyme

There are some things that are as much fun to do when you are seventy as when you were seven. Going barefoot is not one of them. It took me a while to figure out why. It's largely a matter of weight. When you weigh fifty pounds you can run across a gravel driveway with minimum discomfort, but when one hundred thirty-five pounds are bearing down on the tender soles of your feet the gravel might as well be a bed of coals.

A symbol of summer to me as a child was when I could go barefoot. It wasn't acceptable in the suburbs, except in your own backyard, but as soon as we got to Maine for the summer my first act after scrambling out over the bulging baggage rack on the Studebaker touring car was to untie my small brown Coward oxfords, pull off my socks and race across the lawn of Cloverslope in Hinckley. Do you remember the soothing caress of moist grass under your feet, the cool, rough texture of granite doorsteps and the smooth, wide planks of a country kitchen floor?

Of course there were moments of pain those first days, but that was a sort of trial by fire, a rite of passage into summer. If the meadow between Cloverslope and Applehurst (the other farmhouse where my friend Jeanie Porter spent the summer) had just been mowed, the dash across that field held all the elements of walking on glass shards as the sharp stubble stabbed my feet. But that was short-lived. Our feet soon became tough and leathery and immune to most pain.

There was an alternate route. I could run around the field on the dirt road which was longer but it was pure delight to feel the soft powdery dust cushion my feet. If it had rained it was silky-brown mud, like chocolate pudding, that squished between your toes and oozed over the tops of your feet. My mother, tolerant of most things, seemed to me to be very unreasonable in insisting that I wash my feet in a tin basin by the doorstep before going to bed. My feet looked clean enough to me after I had wiped them off on the grass. But at least after washing them I could admire my stained and calloused soles. It was a matter of pride to lose your tenderfoot status as quickly as possible.

Those summers were spent inland on the Kennebec River but we did get to the seashore now and then. When we visited my grandparents in Los Angeles one year I couldn't believe that the California sand could be so blistering hot when the water of the Pacific was so icy cold, colder than the Atlantic off the coast of Maine. At the New Jersey shore my bare feet felt the contrast between the deep, dry sand where we parked our blankets, lunch and parents, the wet, hard-packed sand at the shoreline and the sucking, dark sand under the water.

When I was ten years old I went to Michigan with my father while he attended a conference on the east shore of Lake Michigan. It was held at a summer campsite right on the dunes. I couldn't believe that Lake Michigan was a lake and not an ocean. I couldn't see across it. There were steamers as big as ocean liners on the horizon and the waves curled and broke like the combers at the New Jersey shore. But there was no tide and the water was not salty. Most amazing of all, the sand not only squeaked, it sang! The other children and I scuffed across it to make it sing louder and we slid down the musical dunes that were as high as small hills back home. I was used to having the sun rise over the water and set over the land but here it was just the opposite, a reversal of the order so familiar to an eastern child that I had accepted it as universal.

A few years ago when I read about a local boy who developed a lucrative business of retrieving golf balls from a pond on the Kwiniaska golf course in Shelburne by feeling for them in the mud with his toes, I could feel that mud between my own toes but it evoked an unsettling memory. I remember wading into the shallow water at the edge of a lake to pick water lilies. The water was thick with reeds and eel grass, as well as water lily plants. The squishy mud and long slippery stems of the water lilies conjured up images of tentacles of unknown aquatic creatures curling around my ankles. The next time I picked water lilies I did it from

68

a canoe. But that is not without risk of another sort. The flower is firmly attached to the root by a stem as long as six feet. You lean over and pull gently, then harder, but one yank too hard will land you right back in that aqueous jungle.

Now my barefoot moments are minimal by choice. No more stepping on painfully sharp shells at the seashore or slipping on the rounded stones on the shores of Lake Champlain. I don't miss the inevitable stubbed toes and splinters of my childhood or aspire to calloused soles. My pleasure in being barefoot is restricted to the last moment before getting into bed at night and the first moments of getting out of bed in the morning when I sink my toes deep in the thick sheepskin rug at my bedside and revel in the warmth and luxury of four inches of pure wool.

This One's for the Birds

The expression, "Crazy as a loon," undoubtedly comes from the maniacal sound of the loon's cry rather than from any aberrant action on the loon's part. The loon is not a crazy mixed-up bird. He can outwit his predators or nosy humans by diving and swimming underwater for unbelievably long distances and periods of time. But the loon does have a physical rather than a psychological problem. His legs, set back so far, make great oars and rudders, but he is virtually helpless on shore. In fact he can't become airborne except by pattering on the water, flapping his wings wildly while heading into the wind. Like a plane, he needs flying speed to lift his heavy body. When he lands he splats down on his chest in the water like the belly flops of my childhood.

Fran Howe, the Bird Lady on the tv program "Across the Fence," told about a loon found on top of Mount Mansfield that was unable to take off without the necessary body of water. Fortunately, this was reported to the game warden who wrapped the bird carefully, transported it to a nearby lake and set it on the water. If it hadn't been rescued it certainly would have died. But why did the loon land on the mountain? It surely knew better. Perhaps the bird was forced down in one of the violent windstorms we had early in the summer. The loons spend the winter on coastal waters so they do fly over the mountains every fall, but if they break their journey it is on one of the lakes on the way.

Anyway, it's a nice story. People are crazier than loons. We condone the shooting of wild geese and ducks but go to extraordinary lengths to rescue an injured fowl. Our mores apparently indicate that instant death is acceptable but it is considered cruel to leave a bird to die slowly. Maybe that's not so crazy. We aren't that humane in dealing with our own kind. I'd prefer instant death, wouldn't you? Of course it would be even nicer to have the counterpart of a kindly forest ranger transplant me to an environment where I could function independently once more.

Another bird at odds with the environment was the wild turkey who was troubling the motorists in Stowe last summer. For two months this turkey crossed Vermont Rte 100 north of Stowe village, eluding residents and game officials trying to remove him from the path of oncoming cars. Cars were slamming on their brakes to avoid hitting him. Game warden Eric Nuse, and Lillian Ricketson, whose farm was the turkey's headquarters, had tried a variety of entrapment plans with no success. Nuse had grain donated by Lamoille Grain Co. and was soaking it in whiskey and gin hoping to get the turkey drunk and capture him while he was under

71

the influence, but the turkey was struck and killed by a truck during a heavy rainstorm.

I always thought the pecking order was just for the birds and the armed forces. But when our grandsons Patrick, eleven, and Peter, nine, were in Vermont last summer they spent a lot of time with their cousin Morgan Page who is six. For the most part they played amicably enough but occasionally their priorities were in conflict. One day Patty (mother of Patrick and Peter) heard Peter explaining the pecking order to wide-eyed Morgan. "You see, Patrick is older than I am so that's why he bosses me. I'm older than you so I can boss you."

Morgan, not altogether convinced by this logic, was not about to accept his status without protest. "But who can I boss?"

Peter thought about it for a while and then remembered that Morgan has another cousin, on his father's side, who was ten months old. "Oh you can be the boss of Michael. You're *lots* bigger and older than he is."

Might may not always be right but it does rivet your attention.

Morgan and I shared a unique bird sighting last winter when he was spending a night with us. The next morning he and I went to Desso's store (Mecca for all grandchildren in Chittenden East) to get the Sunday *New York Times* for George, chocolate peppermints for Morgan, and a chance for me to show off Morgan to Lil Desso. As we turned the corner from Nashville Road onto Brown's Trace, a loud squawk made us look up into a broken-off stump of an old maple and there was an enormous pileated woodpecker, as big as a crow but sleeker, more tapered and with that distinctive scarlet crest. He ignored us completely and went on excavating a two-foot-long hole in the trunk. The chips that fell at the base of the tree were as big as walnuts and the sound of his relentless quest for carpenter ants could have been heard for half a mile. Morgan's big blue eyes and mouth were wide open in amazement. He is familiar with downy and hairy woodpeckers at his own bird feeders but this impressive bird stunned him into momentary silence. When we finally went on our way he muttered softly, "Woodpeckers grow much bigger in Jericho."

Since we had some of the pine trees removed near the house we have had no downy or hairy woodpeckers at the feeders. There is still plenty of nearby cover. Is there a connection? Also, this winter we've had the return of redpolls, sometimes thirty at a time at the niger seed feeder Debbie gave us for Christmas. A few years ago we put out niger seed and it was ignored. This year, ten days after we put out the niger seed, they began to come—four then twelve then three dozen. They are not as tame as chickadees but the males' rosy breasts and their tiny red berets are bright against the mounds of snow.

More Small World

I'm always surprised at the number of small coincidences that illuminate our lives. How did I happen to look out of the window at just the moment when four baby blue jays wobbled on the edge of their nest and took their first wobbling leaps into the wide world of the nearby branches? Or that four-year-old Henry Kite, whom I taught in nursery school in Greenwich Village in 1939, would turn out to be a neighbor in Jericho Center forty years later.

But the most unusual coincidence happened last year. When I was eight years old, spending the winter in Geneva, Switzerland, a young German-Swiss woman, Olga Hausman, was our cook and dish-breaker. I say that advisedly. She had a heavy hand with fragile objects. She returned to the United States with us and lived with my family for a year before going to California to seek her fortune in Hollywood. A few years later she returned to Switzerland to care for her aging parents. My mother heard from her occasionally, but after my mother died in 1963 Olga slipped out of my life.

The year after Olga went to California an eighteen-year-old young friend from Maine, Alice Cain, came to live with my family and continue her education. Alice later taught school, married, moved to Hoosick Falls, New York and had two daughters, Anne and Joyce. A few years ago Alice Cain Bordeaux moved to Vermont and we renewed our friendship. In the meantime, her daughter Joyce had moved to Switzerland and was living in a small village, Yverdon, near the French border. One day Joyce was sitting on a park bench and got into a conversation with a very old Swiss woman who recognized Joyce as American and told her that long ago she had gone to America with an American family and had lived in New Jersey in a town called Montclair. Joyce told her that that was very strange because her mother had once lived in Montclair with a family named Hurrey and their daughter, Marguerite, now lived near her mother in Vermont. Olga recalled how Marguerite, just a little girl, had gone to the farmer's market in Geneva with her each day and used to grind the coffee for her in the hand grinder in the kitchen.

"My name is Olga Hausman. I am now over ninety years old. That time was sixty-three years ago and I haven't heard of that family in twenty years."

Joyce wrote to her mother who 'phoned me and I wrote at once to Olga, sending her a snapshot I had of her with my family in 1922. She sent me a picture of herself in 1985, just in time. Olga died in May of 1986.

Now let's hear you top that for a chance meeting on a park bench!

If we had used only first names, a current custom I deplore, this coincidence never would have come to light. What's in a name? I'll tell you what's in my name. I am, and I like it to represent me as a total person. I know it's a foible of my generation, but I really don't like a gum-chewing clerk at a doctor's office, who never saw me before in her life, calling me Maggie. I am perfectly happy to have my sons-in-law call me Maggie and I wouldn't mind if my grandsons called me that instead of Grandma, but I still think the dignity of Mrs. Wolf is appropriate in a professional setting.

I am equally out of style in disliking the use of only my last name. If I am mentioned in the newspaper, after the first mention I become Wolf thereafter. It makes me sound like a hockey coach—too macho, too impersonal. Recently a beloved and distinguished English teacher in Barre celebrated her one hundredth birthday. The *Times-Argus* gave it a nice write-up and picture but as is now journalism's wont, Miss Faith Linsley was called simply Linsley after the first mention of her name. I can't believe she was comfortable with that.

Sometimes the name you are called on the 'phone reveals when it was that the caller first knew you. If anyone calls me Ita it is a close relative. This was a family nickname, a contraction of Margarita because my parents spent several years in Argentina before I was born and used a few Spanish diminutives. If someone calls me Miggs I know it is a childhood friend from Montclair, New Jersey. If I am called Jiggs it is a college classmate. Because George calls me Maggie I've been Maggie for the past forty-five years. Whatever happened to Marguerite? It's my real name but one I hear so seldom that I do a double take and look behind me to

76

see who is being addressed. The only ones who use it are Ellen Hensel because of her operatic background and fondness for Faust, and Alice Bordeaux who lived with my family when I was a little girl.

Neither George nor I cared much for our middle names so we didn't give our daughters any. In grade school they thought this was a deprivation so Debbie invented one temporarily. Many people dislike their names, or are urged to change them. When Ferdinand Friendly Wachenheimer started working in television the man who hired him announced, "OK, from here on in you're Fred Friendly" and he was and is. Certain ethnic names are difficult if you are from a different culture. Icelandic and Welsh names are my undoing. Can you spell the name of the president of Iceland at the time of Reagan's visit? Vigdis Finnbogadotter, and one of their mountains is Hvannadashnukur.

My paternal grandfather's name was Barzillai Hurry, honest! But my uncle Clarence was teased about the name Hurry when he was a college student and had it changed to Hurrey to make it less like a verb and more like a name. My father, being the younger brother, went along with the change, so in the cemetery in Tecumseh, Michigan there are two Hurreys and two Hurrys. That same uncle was in a law firm in Washington, D.C. with the title of Hurrey and Roper. At another time it was even worse—Hurrey, Ketcham and Roper! When I was a child we had a black laundress named Retha Green and her best friend was Shada Brown.

What's in a name? Quite a lot. A rose by the name of skunk cabbage does NOT smell as sweet.

Why Can't a Man Be More like a Woman?

I've aired my notions about this before in two other books, but fundamental differences between men and women keep popping up. We all know that men and women are different. And never mind exclaiming, "Vive la différence!" I'm not talking about anatomy. I'm talking about the fact that when you hear a man say, "Women are a mystery to me", he really means a woman doesn't see things in black and white like he does. Therefore he's right and she's wrong. (How about *that* for black and white?) At the same time a woman thinks, "He only sees things in black and white. Why can't he see the variations and nuances in color and feeling, in detail, like I do?"

Right or wrong, I don't care to enlist in James Thurber's war between men and women. I'm for peaceful coexistence. But once in a while I notice that my husband, who is much more understanding and intelligent than most men, has a few blind spots and muffled ears where my vision and hearing are clearest, and yet he can grasp a concept in areas where I am just plain dense.

He can figure out how to put an unassembled appliance into functioning order when my palms sweat as soon as I read, "Place rod A into slot B as shown in the above diagram." Yet he said he had never heard of "Herb" of Burger King fame, though that commercial had been aired *ad nauseam* during tv programs that he had been watching. He neither knows nor cares that Nancy Reagan's favorite color is red, that Maria Shriver is the daughter of Jean Kennedy and Sargent Shriver, what my dress size is, or the names of his first cousins. He hasn't the foggiest idea who his fourth-grade teacher was, while I clearly recall the red hair, fierce expression and tortoise-shell glasses that distinguished Miss Whitlock.

All right, so he is not in pursuit of trivia. Well I'd like to believe that's not my aim either but why do those minutiae stick in my head? The difference doesn't make either of us right or wrong. It is just that our tune-out buttons function in different areas.

I think some of these differences are universal. Take old clothes for instance, and I wish you'd take some of George's. I'll bet a Masai warrior doesn't want to part with his frayed loincloth any more than George wants to part with a golf shirt that is so full of holes it could be used to pan gold. Most women like to discard old clothes. Several of my friends have admitted to a recurring fantasy of giving away all their old clothes and buying a whole new wardrobe. Most men will cling to a threadbare cardigan or a weathered trench coat as though it was a sniffy blanket. It probably is.

My husband is a physician. He can spot Bell's palsy at twenty paces but he doesn't notice that a neighbor is pregnant. He knows right away if I am worrying about a grandchild, but I had to tell him when I got my hair colored.

Morgan, who insisted on dressing himself at a very early age, was perfectly content with his shirt on backwards and unmatching socks. He did like his shoes to be on the correct feet but only because "they run funny" if they're not. When Debbie, his mother, was that age she would insist that I tie and retie her red shoes until the laces were so tight that I wondered about the circulation to her toes. At a somewhat older age both of our daughters would spend hours on and off the 'phone trying to decide what to wear to school the next day.

My most cherished example of the clothes-unconscious father was the day Wally Riker took Donald to nursery school, back in the '40s when we all lived in New York City. Wally later became chairman of the Department of Pharmacology at Cornell Medical College, but at that time he was just out of his residency. The only reason that Wally was nursemaiding was that his wife Ginny was in the delivery room at the Lying-In Hospital, hoping that their number two child, who turned out to be Walter Jr., would speed up his entrance into the world.

While Wally was stuffing Donald into his snow jacket Donald protested that it didn't feel right. All the way to school he fussed that the jacket hurt. Wally tuned out the complaints and handed him over to his teacher who, helping Donald out of his jacket, looked up at his father and asked, "Does he always wear a large wooden coat hanger under his jacket?"

Another Odd Couple

Moose are not common in Vermont and when one does go public it is something of a conversation piece. The Vaughans in Cambridge were unwilling hosts to a moose in their swimming pool a few years back. It didn't do the moose or the lining of the swimming pool any good. And another moose wandered into a playground in Burlington, which is abnormal behavior for such a reclusive animal.

In the fall of 1986 the equally unusual three-way gubernatorial campaigns of Madeleine Kunin, Peter Smith and Bernie Sanders had to share front-page space with Jessica, a small Hereford cow, and her unlikely would-be lover, a bull moose.

There is no doubt that love is blind. The cow, Jessica, a resident of Larry Carrara's farm in Shrewsbury, didn't look like a female moose to anyone except Bullwinkle, her 800-pound admirer. But he was tireless in his pursuit of her affection. For three weeks he never left her side, nuzzling her amorously and resting his huge head on her broad, unresponsive back in a determined effort to convince her that all is fair in love and war.

Now Parker's Gore, near Shrewsbury, is not the corner of 42nd Street and Fifth Avenue. And the people in that area want to keep it that way. In fact they hope that the presence of the love-struck moose and the resulting publicity will help their efforts to preserve Parker's Gore and prevent development. The moose seems to them an appropriate symbol of the wildness they would like to protect. But during the moose-mating season in October and early November hundreds of cars, more than 1,000 people, and some of the news media, including Cable News, the *New York Times*, television crews and an Australian radio station focused on this odd couple. The onlookers stood at a minimally respectful distance, restrained by an orange tape barrier, cameras in hand, watching the moose's futile attempts to win Jessica's approval. No luck. Maybe she was turned off by Bullwinkle's large snout and enormous rack of lethal-looking antlers. His image was certainly impressive but hardly romantic. Maybe her hormones reacted negatively to the voyeurism of the crowd. After all, a cow who has become accustomed to the relative privacy of artificial insemination may not respond to the call of the wild. She made it quite clear that she regarded him only as a friend. He may have been a lot of bull but she was a cow of a different color. She had no intention of trading her Hereford companions and a warm barn in winter for life in a swamp with a fellow who likes to stand knee-deep in a lily pond.

It may have been a disappointing season for the moony

moose but Larry Carrara, the owner of the object of Bull-winkle's affection, turned his pasture into new green in November. He had T-shirts made bearing the legend, "The Moose is Loose on Carrara's Mt. in Shrewsbury, Vt.", sold them for $8 apiece and hoped that the moose would stay in the rut overtime.

Is there something about Vermont that produces ill-starred love affairs among its fauna? A few years ago neighbors of the Hensels in Underhill witnessed the efforts of a Canada goose to win the heart of a plastic, inflated dolphin on the Hensels' pond. The goose spent the entire summer guarding, cajoling, and wooing the toy and didn't give up until the dolphin "died" from multiple, unmendable leaks.

Fall

October

After the drowsinesss and occasional, in Vermont, mugginess of summer, October is a clarion call to the senses. You can hear it in the baying of a skein of geese flying south, in the rumble of the school bus, the chatter of a red squirrel scolding, and the rustle of the dry cornstalks when you are finding the last small pumpkin hidden in the grass at the edge of the garden.

"By Jeesum, I'm jest standin' here smellin' October," an elderly Vermonter remarked to himself as he stood in an apple orchard admiring the heavily-laden trees. Asters and chrysanthemums, piles of leaves, the inside of a pumpkin. You can shut your eyes and smell this vibrant season.

You can feel it in the crunch of frost on the brittle grass underfoot, on the smooth, cool rind of a pumpkin and the sharp bite of early morning air soon to be mellowed by the warmth of the Indian summer sun.

You can taste it in the spurt of apple juice as you bite into a just-picked Northern spy apple, in the green tomato and cabbage relish you just ladled into the jars, in the mashed buttercup squash blended with butter. Its deep gold is the color of October, not spring's tender young green-gold, but the ripe orange-gold of pumpkins, goldenrod and, most of all, the golden maples. Suddenly, in the second week of October all the sugar maples turn to gold, shading from a touch of chartreuse at the base to *National Geographic*-cover yellow at the top. Many of the leaves are scarlet tipped. It is luminous in the golden tree tunnels and in sharp contrast to the dark green pines and hemlocks, the same contrast you see in the Rockies—golden aspens with dark evergreens. On every doorstep there is a pumpkin, sometimes joined by stuffed Halloween scarecrows in reclining funny positions. Bunches of Indian corn hang in the front doors, and in our storeroom mesh bags of onions are hung above the bags of potatoes. Squash are piled on the floor and jars of pickles and jellies stand at attention in rows along the shelves. It is a time of gathering and storing and preparing for the winter while still savoring the warmth of Indian summer.

November

While visiting Patty in early November we went to the Morris Arboretum. There had been no frost yet in eastern Pennsylvania and roses were still in bloom. Swans were drifting among the fallen leaves on a pond. A huge ginkgo tree, at least twenty-five feet high, with its delicate fan-shaped leaves reminded me that ginkgoes were around when dinosaurs roamed the earth. A Chinese paper maple looked as though it was shedding its whole outer skin, showing the

85

red-gold underbark. There were holly trees and smooth-skinned, softly-wrinkled beech trees, the bark the color of an elephant's hide. It was like being in a foreign country because of the many species that I never had seen before.

Back in Vermont we can still pick lettuce and brussels sprouts, so good this year with cheese sauce. George would eat shingles with cheese sauce. Carrots and beets still in the garden. I put the carrots in plastic bags in the refrigerator and they stay crisp and fresh until March.

We have started to fill the bird feeders again but the birds are slow to come back, a few chickadees, blue jays and downy woodpeckers.

November 14. Eight inches of snow yesterday. Very heavy on the pines, but the snow brought the birds, including one purple finch, to the feeders. Lots of ducks on Shelburne Bay. Our weatherman said that November is our greyest month, with only 30% of possible sunshine. The last three days bear him out, not a glimmer of sunshine. Why does 32° in November feel so much colder than 10° in January? Maybe for the same reason that Lake Shore Drive in Chicago or the boardwalk in Atlantic City feel much colder at 32° than other places with the same temperature—the dampness, the lack of snow on the ground, and the leaden skies reflected in the leaden water draining the spirit. Even the geese are depressed and a little confused. At this time of year we often hear and then see a skein of Canada geese flying south. It is a lovely wild sound often compared to sleigh bells or called "the baying of the hounds of heaven." But there have been reports that some are flying north again. Returning to familiar ground while the weather is stormy?

November 23. Just returned from visiting the Rowleys in

Florida. It was beautifully balmy while we were there, although since we returned they have had a bad hurricane on the panhandle. Scarlet hibiscus were in bloom with yellow butterflies hovering over them. All of their citrus trees were killed by the cold last year but they have planted more. Sam took us in his boat twenty miles up the St. Johns river to Jacksonville. It is such a wide river that it is astonishing to read the depth meter, ranging from seven to almost twelve feet in the middle. Coots and cormorants, an occasional egret or blue heron. To my delight but their dismay there was a twelve-foot alligator in the water right near their dock. The Rowleys don't swim off their dock but their neighbors do, so they have to tell the Fish and Game Department to come and remove the alligator. Only his big knobby head showed above the water.

When Sam took us up Black Creek, there was one dead tree that had thirty-two black vultures roosting on its branches for the night. They are so ominous looking—small naked heads incongruous on top of the big black bodies and wide wingspread. Why do they seem so sinister to us? Is it because we know they feed on carrion and will circle over a dying animal for hours?

Big turtles catching the late afternoon sun were basking on logs and slid off into the water as we passed.

The sweet gum trees, their maple-like leaves turned red, contrasted with the grey-green live oaks and the glossy dark green magnolias.

It is swampy land, strange and inhospitable to a Vermonter, but fun to watch from the comfort of the boat. Not much small-bird sound or activity in November, but back at the Rowleys' houses there were cardinals at their bird feeder competing with big grey squirrels that make our little red squirrels look like pigmies.

Jane saw a bald eagle but I missed it.

November 24. Hunting season nearly over and I'm always glad. I have no quarrel with a man who hunts for a deer to provide food for his family as well as for the pleasure of being out in the early winter woods. And I know that the deer would be too numerous and some would die of starvation if the herds were not thinned. What I dislike are the cars often parked just up the road from our house with about four red-jacketed, scruffy-looking men sitting in them drinking beer. It's not safe to walk in our woods during hunting season. These Nimrods are apt to shoot at anything that moves. Of course we always say they are from out-of-state, but unfortunately the license plates often are marked Vermont.

November 28, Thanksgiving. Snowing lightly with about two inches on the ground. Phoned Patty in Ambler, Pennsylvania, and it is raining there. Last year we ate our last home-grown turkey. It had been frozen for a year and was fine. We've found that the advice on how long to keep frozen foods is more conservative than necessary for us. We've had a pork roast that has been frozen for a year and five months with no noticeable change in texture or flavor. The sliced bacon begins to lose its best flavor after a few months, but we store most of it in unsliced one-pound squares and it keeps well for a year.

I'm looking at a hairy woodpecker at the suet feeder, upside down but with his tail at right angles to his body. When he is right side up he always uses his broad tail as a brace against the feeder or a tree trunk.

We are being outwitted by mice. We have never had them in the house before, although we have them every fall in the storage area over the utility room and in the utility room where the washer and drier are. They consume large quantities of D-con and each fall we catch several in regular mouse traps, but this year they are taking the bait out of the traps without springing them. I can understand how they can do this with a bit of cheese but how do they remove a smear of peanut butter without springing the trap? Today when I looked in the back of the silver drawer in the kitchen there was a whole cache of grain and seeds in one corner and the tarnish-retardant cloth was chewed in several spots. There are mouse droppings on the pots and pans shelf too. This calls for sterner measures!

November 30. I am half ashamed to admit that we set out one of those mouse traps that is made of some very sticky stuff that mires them down. We caught two that way and George disposed of them because I couldn't bear to. A dead mouse in a spring trap is one thing but a live one with shining little eyes is quite another. The news must have been spread through the mouse grapevine because we've seen no more since.

Wreathed in Smiles

Deck the halls with boughs of holly, mistletoe, balsam, cedar, bay leaves or, if you have that much use for chili peppers, you can order a wreath from the southwest made entirely of tiny, hot, red peppers. Of course it would take your remaining years to use that many red peppers unless your cuisine was limited to Mexican entrees, but the wreath would look pretty and I'll bet the birds would leave it alone.

When we first came to Vermont I was surprised to see Christmas wreaths, faded and khaki-colored, still hanging on many front doors in April. Wherever I had lived before, the Christmas wreath came down with the Christmas tree and was carted off by the trash man. But a few winters in Vermont and a fervent wish to be forgiven for having been born a flatlander convinced us that our wreath too should stay up at least until Easter. Sometimes it even drooped there until it was displaced by the Indian corn we grew in the garden for fun and profit. The fun was pulling back the husks and being surprised by the spectrum of colors. Some were mahogany, rose and white, purple and greyish blue, or yellow with chestnut brown. The profit was small but a gratifying bonus when the local florist bought any we could spare.

But back to wreaths. From the leis of Hawaii to the laurel wreaths of Greece and Rome the wreath has symbolized continuity of life and faith. That's why evergreens were used, and they still are, but now there are many other kinds.

Debbie makes wreaths from grapevines or a circular base of straw in which she fastens dried flowers and grasses. Patty made me an aromatic herb and spice wreath with little bundles of cinnamon sticks, peppercorns, bay leaves and star anise on a straw base covered with flowered material. George's father was skillful at making a wreath by bending a metal coathanger into a circle and tying the evergreens and pine cones to the wire.

When Joan and Jack Cross moved to Jericho from Montreal, Jack thought our habit of leaving our wreath moldering on our door was ridiculous if not downright lazy. He threatened to take ours to the dump if we lacked the energy. We clung to it stubbornly, but when we were away for a few days and they were feeding our chickens, they brought over their wreath and ran it up our flagpole. So of course when they went to Europe the next spring we felt obliged to take our very weary wreath and put it on their roof. One year we hung it on the tool house next to their swimming pool. It was a little bit difficult to explain to the young man who was painting their house that this was not vandalism. His bewilderment showed that he was not a Vermonter. Vermonters don't question the aberrations of those "from away." They are more to be pitied than censured. In our early years in Vermont when I asked a neighbor why he hadn't told me I should wait till Memorial Day to put in the garden, his answer was simply, "You didn't ask."

Home for Christmas

The only part of Dickens' *Christmas Carol* that I really like is Christmas dinner with the Cratchits. All that other dreary business about Marley's ghost and Scrooge is too depressing for a season that is supposed to be merry. But I love the gathering of the Cratchit clan, the goose redolent of sage and onions and the plum pudding knocking against the side of its pot. Right there you have my three ingredients for the ideal Christmas dinner—a family, a goose and a plum pudding. We raised geese for several years, and not to be outdone by the Cratchits, we had goose for dinner at least three times. The first time it was a bit tough and stringy but we chomped on it loyally because no one would dare to complain on Christmas. By the next Christmas I had consulted several cookbooks, and after marinating and braising the goose was delicious, if a bit skimpy in the number of servings compared to a turkey. Now that we no longer raise geese or turkeys we have decided that roast beef is what Wolfs and Cratchits really would prefer when they could afford it.

As for the gathering of the clan, Patty and her husband, Tage Ström, lived in Finland and Denmark for fourteen years and their boys, Patrick and Peter, then ages eight and six, had never spent a Christmas in the United States. In the winter of 1984-85 they were in Ambler, Pennsylvania. One of the selling points to Patrick, who wanted to return to Denmark, was that they could come to Vermont for Christmas with us in Jericho. We would provide snow, cut down the tree from our woods, hang up their stockings at the fireplace and have a Dickensian feast. Debbie, Steve, and Morgan Page live relatively nearby and usually come out Christmas Day unless they go to Steve's parents' in Chevy Chase. So the head count was nine—George and I, our two daughters, their husbands and the three grandsons.

Patrick and Peter had notified us in advance that we must wait to get the tree until they arrived the day before Christmas. Off the Ströms trudged up our hill with saw and hatchet and varying mental pictures of what the tree should look like. Our house is small and I had hinted that a modest tree would do very nicely. I had even climbed up the hill a few weeks before and tagged a couple of six-foot trees that I thought they might like. They had been gone a long time when I heard George exclaim, "My Lord, look what they've got!" It was Birnam Wood coming to Dunsinane with the whole little army of Tage, Patty, Patrick, and Peter completely hidden behind a fourteen-foot hemlock with a wing spread of about ten feet. But according to Patrick it was "the most beautiful tree in the whole world", and after considerable pruning of lower limbs it was forced through the door and mounted with the help of a few guy wires and six pairs of hands.

The next step, my least favorite, was putting the lights on the tree. I have nothing against Christmas-tree lights on other people's trees. It is just that at our house George always cons me into draping them on the tree and then never lets me turn them on. Well, not *never* exactly, but after I plug them in I don't have time to stand back and admire the effect before he suggests turning them off. The hot bulbs might be touching the needles. Dry needles burn like tinder and the tree might catch fire. The argument that this tree hasn't been off its root stock more than an hour and is standing in water doesn't even calm his fears the first day. We've never had a tree ignite. How could we? The lights are never on long enough even to warm the needles! I can dimly remember a Christmas in my early childhood when we had real candles in those little metal holders that clamped on the branches. I also remember my mother's anxiety and my father standing by with a bucket of sand . It may have been beautiful but it wasn't relaxing. Even I, whom George regards as a latent pyromaniac, wouldn't want to play with that much fire.

Patrick had made stained glass ornaments for the tree. Peter contributed a dreidel made of Play-Doh and a set of pictures explaining what the unfamiliar Hebrew markings meant. The boys decorated the tree as high as they could reach and even Tage, who is tall, had to stand on a step stool to hang the few ornaments that the boys were willing to spare to adorn the top branches.

Patty's family was sleeping at Debbie and Steve's house Christmas Eve so it wasn't until Christmas Day that we learned of Peter's concern about Santa Claus. In Finland

and Denmark Joulupukki comes to the door the day before Christmas and asks if the children have been good enough to warrant gifts. The year before, the sight of this all-powerful one was too much for Peter who only dared to peek around the corner of the door. But Patrick assured us that while *he* was a model of good behavior, "Peter's not very good. He bites." Fortunately, that was just one small man's opinion and Peter received his share of the loot.

But in America Peter found different customs. He waited all Christmas Eve afternoon and evening for Santa Claus to show up and finally voiced his anxiety. They assured him that the American Santa Claus comes in the night. After all three boys were asleep Steve made a tape, complete with "Ho, Ho, Ho's", calling the boys by name to convince them that Santa Claus really had been there. In the morning Peter and Morgan listened in awe to the tape, but Patrick, full of the sophistication of his eight years, said, "You know, the American Santa Claus sounds a lot like Steve."

They arrived at our house, the older boys resplendent in navy-blue blazers, dress shirts and ties and Morgan in a scarlet velour jump suit, a vision better than sugar plums to dance through a grandmother's head. We all squeezed around the table, with Morgan perched on the step stool. The floor was knee-deep in wrappings and toys but miraculously no toy was broken and no feelings hurt. There were small candles in little holders on the table which Morgan recognized as birthday candles and shouted "Whose birthday?" When told it was Jesus's birthday, three-year-old Morgan burst into "Happy birthday, baby Jesus" and insisted that we all sing to the birthday child. The boys' table manners were impeccable or at least a reasonable facsimile thereof, the roast beef was rare and the pudding gave off an aroma to warm the cockles of Mrs. Cratchit's heart. I gratefully bequeathed the ritual of flaming the brandy to Tage, and after an abortive start he produced the best halo of blue flames we've ever had. We toasted the absent grandparents, Gunne and Hasse Ström in Finland and Alyce and Russel Page in Chevy Chase.

In the silence of repletion I seemed to hear the echo of a small voice whispering, "God bless us everyone."

The following year Patty and her family were still in America and so they were able to come for Christmas again. This time we already had set up and decorated a more modest tree. No one compared it unfavorably to the previous giant of the forest. In fact, in their eagerness to explore the mysterious packages underneath, it wasn't mentioned at all.

There was a lot of admiration for the handmade gifts. Patty and Patrick had carved and painted a lovely little cardinal on a stand. Debbie had made fudge. Peter had made a fat green candle. Patty had woven a beautiful egg basket, and Morgan had made multicolored wrapping paper in pastel colors for the gifts. The Transformers went through their transformations. The sweaters and socks were tried on for size and Morgan, up to his chin in wrappings, surfaced long enough to ask, "Any more presents, Grandma?" "No, that's all." "Well, how about wrapping up a few more?" "I don't have any more." "Maybe you could go to the store and buy some."

So much of the excitement of Christmas is in the anticipation. How well I remember that bittersweet moment when Christmas was over, when all the mystery was gone and future holidays—your birthday or next Christmas—were too remote for comfort.

Unfortunately we've grown accustomed to surfeit. The grandsons have far more toys than our children had and our children had far more than we had. A generation farther back, my father told me that one of the big excitements of Christmas when he was a boy in Michigan was an orange in his sock, a rare treat in the 1880s. His other gifts were hand-knit socks and mittens and perhaps one toy, a wonderful surprise.

It's easy to blame the advertising men and the stores, and I do, but they wouldn't stock those towers of outer space war machines and dried-apple-faced dolls if we didn't get caught up in the frenzy to buy them.

Are children becoming hoarders rather than improvisers? Patrick and Peter collect transformers and figures, coins, baseball cards and monster cards. In the '20s we collected stamps and samples of everything. Our two daughters collected Ginny dolls, their myriad outfits and tiny little figurines. The acquisitive urge is alive and well among the shell gatherers on Sanibel Island. We are still atavistic enough to be hunter-gatherers. But do we have to hunt and gather armed spaceships, horror monsters and devices that destroy the world?

When we were first married I taught nursery school in Greenwich Village. The children were from a variety of economic backgrounds. Most of the parents were actors, artists or industrial designers, but one or two families lived in the Village simply because it was cheap. One little girl came from a very poor family. I was pretty sure they would not have a Christmas tree, so I suggested to her mother that she take home the small one in our classroom because it would go to waste in the empty room over the holidays. They asked me the next day to come to see the tree. They lived in a cold-water flat and it wasn't only the water that was cold. The stairs were rickety and dank and the apartment was heated only by a kerosene stove. But Joan led me proudly to the transformed tree. She and her mother had made silver bangles from cast-off gum wrappers, had cut pictures of ornaments, toys, and cookies from a *Good Housekeeping* magazine they found, and under the tree was a Nativity scene they had cut out of a church calendar. Their pride and delight outshone the towering tree at Radio City.

A few years later, when our two girls were toddlers, we lived in an apartment across from New York Hospital, inhabited by interns, residents and their families. We were all living on very short shoestrings. Interns in those days received no salary, assistant residents got $25 per month and the chief resident $50 per month. Wives with children stayed home and made do. George had started practice so we were relatively affluent, but the habit of penury lingered on and we didn't buy our girls any Christmas presents because they were well-supplied by two sets of grandparents. On the floor below our apartment there was a Mormon couple with two little boys. They lived on almost nothing. The grandparents had sent a small check. Late on Christmas Eve, Alan went out and found a tree for fifty cents while Ruth wrapped the two presents they had bought for the boys—a small inexpensive suitcase each. Their tree was decorated by homemade paper chains and popcorn strings. But all Christmas Day the two little boys played happily, packing and unpacking the suitcases and "going on the train to Salt Lake City" in their double-decker beds. Ruth and Alan had made Christmas magic out of a leftover tree and two modest gifts.

So when it comes to Christmas I find I am a different sort of collector—of memories like Joan's tree and the little suitcases that took Brian and John across the country.

We can't help being bombarded by Christmas hype and hoopla, but we can balance the war toys and other brief fads (do you remember mood rings, pet rocks and Nehru jackets?) with memories that never go to the dump or even to the attic.

I unwrap them each year with the Christmas ornaments, but these images that flash across the inward eye are unbreakable. They can't be burned up by mistake or nibbled by mice, and they don't need to be put away. They return every year and sometimes in between, the true spirits of Christmases past and present, and the hopes for peace to add to them in the future.

January and February

The best thing about January is the promise of spring in the form of seed catalogues that brighten the coffee table and the spirits of that incurable optimist, the gardener. I tell myself that the deep freeze and endless snow are good for the skiers and the orchards, and find my amusement in watching the red squirrels and the birds at our feeders. It is snowing so hard with four inches on the ground and the forecast that it will continue all day. Think I'll stay home.

Patty sent pictures which they took on their return trip to Ambler. She persuaded Tage to get off the turnpike at Montclair, New Jersey to see if she could remember her way to the former homes of both sets of her grandparents. Patty hadn't been to Montclair in twenty years. The houses had long since been sold to other families after George's parents and mine had died, but Patty found both homes and took pictures of them with her boys in front. Such a flood of memories when you see the house in which you were born and where your parents lived for fifty years! How few families live in one house for fifty years now. We have lived in four apartments and seven different houses in forty-seven years and that is far less than many peripatetic households.

January 22. The cold has abated a little. It is now 15° at noon, instead of yesterday's 5°, and the wind is kinder. The pine needles are drooping and stiff, hoarding their juices. There is a foot of new snow on the ground. For the last five days it has snowed almost continuously, fine misty snow that is slow to accumulate.

January 25. In the winter all our roads are potentially hazardous. There are certain spots that I treat with great respect. If I get up Fred Casey's hill and don't meet a car coming down and don't have to shift, I know I'm OK until I reach the pine-shaded curve at the beginning of our land, where the ice doesn't melt all winter, even in a thaw, because the winter sun never reaches it.

I haven't had much experience as a sailor but I can imagine the relief of making it into a snug harbor during a storm. When our roads are bad, either with black ice or blowing whiteouts, it feels like a real achievement to make it into my own garage. And after I have waded through knee-deep snow down to the barn to feed the chickens, and then refilled the bird feeders, the warm house wraps around me like a down comforter. It is no fun eating unless you are hungry. Maybe we have to feel the need of warmth or safety in order to appreciate it.

I can remember as a child the relief of feeling the solid earth under my feet after I had climbed so high in a tree that I had been really afraid that I couldn't get down. But why do children, or adults for that matter, make themselves do dangerous feats to test their courage? We have a friend who is a serious high-mountain climber, I mean Mount Logan and the Himalayas. When asked why such expeditions lure him so irresistibly, he says because it is so beautiful. I believe that is only part of it. I think that danger brings people close together, makes them acutely aware of their need for each other.

January 27. Mixed-up chickadee singing "Spring soon!" Nellie McClure's one hundredth birthday in 1987. She and Margaret Snyder, ninety-six, live in Nellie's snug white house on Brown's Trace. Meals-on-Wheels delivers two meals a day and Nellie's relatives come over each Sunday and care for the house and lawn in the summer. Both ladies are alert and interested in everything, especially birds, church and the Mary Fletcher School of Nursing, of which Nellie is the oldest alumna. Nellie was delighted with the shower of cards and gifts. Her vision is not good but Margaret reads to her. When I visit a friend in a nursing home I come away depressed. When I visit Nellie and Margaret I smile at their cheerfulness all the way home. Independence, even partial independence, is enormously nourishing. Note to my children: If I live to be ninety please don't do anything for me that I can do for myself!

These are the days of relentless snow, sifting down silently, rounding out all the remaining sharp contours that poke up through the snowdrifts. Every fence post wears a marshmallow. All the barn roofs support a thick layer of frosting. The rustiest metal roof and the fanciest slate or copper ones are camouflaged into equal status for a few months. The blight of old farm machinery and derelict cars is mercifully softened by mounds of white.

When I was a child, snow was the best part of winter, right up there with Christmas. It meant snowmen, a snow fort, the chance to earn fifty cents shovelling the walks, maybe even a half-day of school. Oh that wonderful feeling when your teacher announced that there would be no afternoon session! You danced home through the snow hoping it would never stop. It never entered my head that to my father, walking up hill a mile from the Erie Railroad station, the snow might not be so welcome. How could *anyone* not love the snow? I don't remember snow plows at all. They must have had them, but of course there were few cars on the streets. I can remember the sound of tire chains clanking and that the milkman's horse had some sort of chains on his hooves.

When we lived in New York City clean snow was of short duration. I remember one big snowstorm in the '40s. For once the city was silent. No buses. No cars. It was strange and beautiful. It reminded all of us of snow in the country and we put on our heavy clothes and cavorted in the middle of York Avenue and 70th Street making snow angels. When the children were little any snowstorm sent us hurrying to Central Park to find some clean snow to play in, before the soot and traffic turned it to grey mush.

When I look out at our pine trees laden with snow and the meadow contoured in white curves, I think how thrilled I would have been by this beauty in our city years. But now, while I still enjoy the look of snow and the long blue shadows, it is a mixed blessing. Yesterday the snow had fallen off the barn roof in front of the door. The door wouldn't open and guess where the shovel was—inside the barn! That meant a trip back to the house for George to get another shovel and dig out the door before he could feed the chickens.

The snow blower is a wonderful help for clearing the driveway, especially this new blower with the electric starter. But even with that we can't go anywhere until the driveway has been blown out. We have to dig through the snow and lift off the frozen tarpaulin to pry the logs out of the woodpile.

Deceptive ditches, camouflaged by snow, reach out and suck in a car or two every day. Our friends who cross-country ski are ecstatic over each new snowfall, but George worries about the weight of snow on the roof. We have one of those long-handled extension snow rakes to remove snow from the roof. It is lightweight but its length makes it bend and wave and I feel as though I'm part of a mobile balancing the other end.

January 28. This morning it was 20° below and the air was full of tiny frozen crystals, not snow, sort of frozen mist, little stinging particles. Underfoot the snow squeaked and the pine needle clusters were pendant and rigid. A blue jay at the feeder was fluffed out to twice his size in his down jacket. Only the chickadees were darting in and out in perpetual motion at the feeders. I don't know why their tiny, twiggy legs don't snap off. But their activity is cheering. If they can dart around with enthusiasm at 20° below certainly I can rouse out of my mental hibernation and *do* something useful. Some people are lethargic in summer and positively frenetic in winter. While I don't want to live in the tropics, the deep cold of winter doesn't fill me with energy. It fills me with the desire to finish whatever I have to do outside— feed the chickens, bring in some wood, and get the mail as quickly as possible and then thaw out my fingers and fogged glasses in the welcoming warmth from the woodstove. The warmth of the wood stove is much more comforting than the convected heat from our electrical baseboard units. You'd think that heat would be heat but it's not. Radiant heat is warmer.

January 30. The last three days are probably the only three out of 365 that make me wonder why we choose to live in the backyard of the North Pole. Saturday and Sunday it snowed, more than eight inches on top of the six we already had which had melted in our January thaw to form a thick layer of ice. Sunday it turned into a mixture of snow and freezing rain all day. Woke up at 3 A.M. feeling the ominous cold and silence that means the power is off. We have electric heat, supplemented with a wood stove and a small bottled-gas heater so we were able to keep warm. But without "the electric" there is no refrigerator, no heat in the utility room where the water tanks are, no tv or typewriter, no cooking stove, iron or vacuum cleaner. We cooked a steak on the gas grill on the porch and cooked our other meals on the small top of the wood stove. All day Monday we expected the power to come back on at any moment, but the trees were so heavily bowed down with ice and snow that they had broken and pulled down wires all over northern Vermont. Our water comes from a well, pumped by guess what. So an outage means no water and no light as well as no appliances. Over my feeble protests George invested in a small generator about twelve years ago. We have used it four times. He starts it once a month year-round to remind it of its function. It is very heavy and moves reluctantly but he dragged it through the snow from the garage onto the porch and got it started. It makes a lot of noise and the exhaust fumes require it to be used outdoors, but it is a source of renewed power.

The generator and I have something in common. Each of us can do only one thing at a time. The generator can either activate the pump so we can flush the toilet, or it can heat the toaster oven, or it can run the refrigerator or the tv and one lamp. So we alternate and with every change George had to reattach wires. The room was crisscrossed with a web of yellow and black wires with Kleenex draped over them to call our attention to their presence. Normal life or an unreasonable facsimile thereof was manageable but almost a full-time occupation — lugging wood, stoking the fire, lighting candles, finding a flashlight, and heating water for the chickens because their waterer is heated by an electric rod. The power was out from 3 A.M. Monday until 8:30 P.M. Tuesday, a total of forty-one hours, by far the longest outage we've ever had. George fled to a neighbor's house to have a shower, and our diet relied heavily on soup.

When the power came back on with the lovely hum of the refrigerator and instant sunrise, the luxury surpassed anything Leona Helmsley offers at the Helmsley Palace. My first indulgence was a bath. While the water was running the pump went on but it stayed on longer than was its wont. I called to George to go look at the pump. He protested that I was just being jumpy because of the outage. True, but I persuaded him to look at it anyway. One of the pipes in the utility room had cracked from freezing and little fountains were turning the room into a miniature Versailles. So he turned off everything. Now we had power but no water. I finished my bath — no sense wasting the warm water in the tank. We borrowed a milk can half-full of water from Clarence Manor, and called Cecil Spalding, our neighborhood plumber. Cecil obliged the next day, and while we prayed that there were no other hidden leaks the pump was turned on.

Everything worked! Happy ending? Not so fast. Our 'phone, which had been making peculiar roaring noises and occasionally letting us in on other people's conversations although we are not on a party line, gave up the ghost. The gods of winter wanted to keep us humble a little longer. We apologized for our complacency, were forgiven and the lovely dial tone was once again heard in our 'phone.

February 14. When Morgan was three he was delighted with the box of Valentines I gave him, but he liked to seal one all up with crisscrosses of Scotch tape and carry it around. When I asked him who it was for he said, "For me. You gave them to me." Patty and Tage's boys, Patrick and Peter, celebrated their first Valentine's Day in the United States in 1985 and found the strange American custom confusing. When putting his valentines together for the school party, Patrick, then eight, asked, "Why do they say, 'Be Mine'? If I give them to my friends they can keep them. They don't have to be mine anymore."

Squirreling Away

The red squirrels provide daily entertainment outside our living-room window. Right now we have more than a foot of snow under the bird feeders but the red squirrels pop right out of the snow then disappear down a secret tunnel and explode right up in another spot. It reminds me of a loon diving under water and then surfacing far away, not where you expect it at all. This is on a smaller scale though. And the squirrel's nose and whiskers are hung with snow. It is the white ring around their eyes that make their faces so expressive and big-eyed. When it is cold like this their tails always are curled up over their backs for insulation.

I don't have the same fondness for grey squirrels. We don't have the greys here, but I love these little guys. They and the chickadees in constant motion assure me that our frozen world is still full of life.

There is no such thing as a squirrel-proof bird feeder, bird feeder sales pitches to the contrary. In Kansas we had a six-foot pole with an inverted saucer-like baffle under the feeder. True, it kept the big, red fox squirrels there from climbing up the metal pole to the feeder, but they scampered out to the ends of the branches of a nearby maple tree and leapt six to ten feet to the feeder, often slipping off but once in a few tries clinging long enough to get a paw hold.

Here in Jericho we have our bird feeders suspended from a wire that runs from the house to a small maple. We have a long tube feeder filled with sunflower seeds, a "satellite" round feeder, and a plastic dish feeder that has a rounded plastic lid four inches above the dish. The squirrels leap from the house wall where a window hinge juts out a little to the tube feeder and then hang upside down, tiny hind feet clutching the top of the tube, reaching into the holes of the tube and stuffing the seeds into their mouths. Sometimes they miss and tumble into the snow only to be back a moment later, swinging upside down and hanging on for dear life. We have a big black bin made of hard plastic mounted high on the porch wall. It must hold twenty-five pounds of seeds. It has a handle on the side. When you pull down the handle the chute opens at the bottom and the seeds flow into a square container that you carry to the feeders. The rigid plastic is too smooth for a foothold but a red squirrel somehow chewed a hole at the bottom of the chute and out flowed the seeds onto the floor. He has been outwitted temporarily by a soft plastic garbage bag anchored with a rubber band around the bottom of the bin.

The main supply of seeds is in a big galvanized garbage can in the garage. The lid is anchored down by a wire running across the top of the lid under the lid handle, and twisted into the handles on each side. So far no squirrel, chipmunk or mouse has figured out how to untwist the wire. I'm sure a raccoon could, but would you mind not telling him where we keep the sunflower seeds?

Mrs. Appleyard put a notice on an apple tree in front of her house asking the resident woodchuck to eat the field flowers instead of her cultivated ones. Apparently woodchucks can read and did oblige, but I doubt very much if our red squirrels would pay any attention to a sign. Like many drivers on the interstate they feel that laws apply to other people. How can you begrudge a few sunflower seeds to anyone so persistent? We never see them in the summer months. What do they eat then? My books say seeds, eggs and fungi. Whose eggs? I've never seen a red squirrel eating a mushroom but I'd like to.

When I watch the squirrel hardly two feet away on the other side of the window he looks at me with no apprehension. He would never let me come within ten feet of him outdoors. It gives me a great chance to really study him — the black hairs with red tips on his tail and the length of his whiskers which extend two inches on either side of his mouth. Now that is the equivalent length of chicken wing feathers protruding on either side of my mouth. Why does he need such long antennae?

Joseph Wood Krutch said, "The rare moment is not the moment when there is something worth looking at, but the moment when we are capable of seeing." Our nine-year-old grandson, Patrick, was asked in school to look carefully at a plant, draw a picture of it, observe it closely and then look at it again later. When asked if it had changed Patrick said, "It's older."

Hats

February 22! Washington's birthday, but not celebrated on this day anymore. It is combined with Lincoln's and was celebrated last Monday which wasn't the date either one was born.

Raining, which is unusual here for February, with temperatures in the 40s and the snow shrinking down in embarrassment at this unseasonable weather. I had to look for my rain hat. It's the only hat I own. How shocked my grandmother would be to know that I don't own even an Easter bonnet or a subdued hat to wear to funerals. But while hunting for my plastic excuse for a hat, which my small grandson thinks is a supermarket produce bag, I began to think of the messages that hats convey.

When we were in Europe one spring we found that everyone thought George was German because of his very short haircut. At the folk museum on Bygdoy, near Oslo, we were handed a guidebook in German. The same was true in Ireland so George bought an Irish tweed cap and instantly he was accepted as Irish! We were smiled upon cheerfully as long as he kept his American accent under his Irish hat.

A prince becomes a king when he is crowned. An archbishop becomes a cardinal when the cardinal's crimson hat is placed upon his head. Graduation from college is symbolized by moving the tassel on your mortarboard from right to left. When you enter a contest it is your hat that you toss into the ring.

Hats are symbolic of nationality – Scotch Tam-o-shanter, Basque beret, the women of the Andes in what look like derbies, the elaborate women's headdresses for each Swiss canton – or of status (miters, tiaras, the high hat worn with morning coat and striped trousers by newly-elected politicians, or conversely the freshman beanie to humble the new student and mark him as inferior to the upperclassman). To tip or touch your hat is also to proclaim yourself someone's humble servant.

Hats are also symbols of occupations – the cowboy's Stetson, the nun's coif, the monk's hood (which I've always suspected was primarily to keep the poor tonsured head warm in those dank, cloistered halls). Before supermarkets, when you went to the butcher shop, the butcher always wore a straw hat. It was as standard as the shavings on the wooden floor or the block on which he cut up your order. If he didn't have a straw hat on you might mistake him for a customer. An artist wore a beret. A fisherman's sou'wester and a fireman's hat are not only for protection but part of the accepted uniform. Have you ever seen a policeman when he takes his hat off? He is suddenly an ordinary man. When he

113

removes his hat he removes his authority. Captain Stubing's hat on "Love Boat" enhances his image, not only because it covers his bald head but because it proclaims him the master of the ship.

The high, silk hats and elaborate wigs and coiffures of the 18th century were confections designed to enhance the wearer's prestige. When I was very small my father occasionally wore a top hat and carried a gold-headed cane on a Sunday walk. He walked differently in his role as influential citizen than he did under his fedora, the hat of a weekday nine-to-five commuter.

In the early years of this century women's hats were piled high with feathers, whole birds, cabbage roses and velvet ribbons. When we played dress-up as children we always got out the hatboxes from the attic and tried on our mothers' retired chapeaux, speaking in affected syllables that we considered grown-up conversation.

I take off my non-existent hat to the one member of a women's club I belong to who always wears a colorful hat. I admire her not because of her choice of hats but for her courage to dress independently. Perhaps she wears them because they are *there*, like the Boston dowager who, when asked where she bought her hats, replied, "My dear, I don't *buy* my hats, I *have* them!" (sometimes for generations).

The renovation of the attic from cold storage to playroom or dormitory is partly responsible for the denouement of the hat. Or is it the other way around? If you have a tower of hatboxes you need an attic in which to store them.

I met a man the other day, a distinguished traveller and writer who was wearing many hats. There was only one collapsible tweed hunting hat, which he kept on during lunch in a restaurant, but the adornments on the hatband literally told his life story. Stuck in the band was a tiny gold lion from an African safari, a red lacquer Japanese archway, a Democratic donkey and a Chinese junk. He didn't need to say a word. He was talking through his hat.

Women used to wear veils on their hats to keep them anchored in a strong wind, to hide their grief while in mourning, or perhaps to flirt behind without being too obvious about it. Why don't we wear hats now? Are we less pretentious (high hat), or is it because most of us are wearing more than one hat figuratively, which isn't easy to do literally? Have you tried to balance a chef's toque, a nurse's cap, a mortarboard and a straw garden hat? Forget it. It's still a man's world, but keep this under your hat!

Footprints

During February when there is snow almost every day, the footprints and tracks of yesterday are filled in and smoothed over and a new story is written on the clean surface. I can tell the size of a truck that has turned in our driveway. A snowshoe hare has hopped around our house in the moonlight and a raccoon, roused from his semi-hibernation, has come up from the rock dens near the brook to investigate the suet at the bird feeders.

Imagine the excitement Robinson Crusoe must have felt when, thinking himself the only human on the island, he saw a human footprint in the sand. And the few who have reported finding the huge footprints of the Abominable Snowman also must have experienced both awe and anxiety.

I have no reason to fear the footprints that serve as my country media. Even though we have bear in the hills near us, they are asleep at this time of year. I've never seen one alive. We saw a dead cub at the side of the road a mile east of our house but George was reluctant to let me get out and examine it for fear that Mama bear might be nearby.

The red squirrel tracks stencil a delicate pattern on the deck. Rather than fear, what I feel is regret that I didn't see the deer who walked daintily down the path to drink at our pool or the red fox that skirted the field. Like the morning news on television, I see the unusual events only after they have happened.

But at least in winter I am informed in far greater detail about life, both wild and domestic, on our land. The tracks of the mail carrier's car are fresh. The mail is here. The feline tracks near the barn could be a neighbor's cat, or a feral cat or bobcat.

I have a lot of trouble identifying some animal tracks. The snowshoe hare is easy with his big hind feet placed foremost as he bounds forward. Today on our back deck it was easy for once to identify raccoon prints—the five-toed "hand" of the front foot and the more elongated hindfoot that looks like a baby's footprint. There have been times in the past when I have tried to find a clear print in the garden but had no luck. I know that on occasion we've had woodchucks and raccoons, but by the time our garden is lush enough to attract a woodchuck around the last of June when our peas and beans are well up, the soil is firm enough not to hold a clear print. Unfortunately the news of his visit is all too clearly told in the sheared-off beans and lettuce. I am not one of those who is willing to share our garden produce with the local fauna. Let the woodchucks eat the clover that abounds in the meadow! Let the raccoons continue to eat whatever they eat all the rest of the year except during the corn season. Did either of them push the rototiller, measure the rows or hoe the weeds?

Cross-country skis leave double ribbons embroidered with the dots made by the poles. Snowmobiles leave wide swaths that loop and circle. From the air, the snowcovered fields are patterned with concentric ovals of dark brown where the manure spreader has distributed its burden on the cornfields.

Morgan's chunky little boots leave small ridged prints next to Debbie's and Steve's full-sized ones on the path to their front door. Sometimes there is a fluff of feathers or a few drops of blood in an indentation where a hawk found his supper, and up in our woods I have seen tufts of rabbit fur under a tree where an owl has hung the rest of a carcass for a later meal.

During the unusually snowy winter of 1987 our snow was two feet deep and holding. No thaw. No January thaw. No February thaw. In fact, one night the red line in our thermometer shrank to 35° below zero, almost out of sight. Our driveway had to be plowed eight times in six weeks. Raccoons and skunks sensibly stayed holed up in their tree houses or caves. Deer must have yarded up in the deep woods. The woodchucks and chipmunks were sound asleep. But the frenetic little red squirrels came popping up out of their sub-snow tunnels reaching up on their hind legs, paws pressed against their chests to peer around at their white world. Their tiny feet made the only animal tracks under the bird feeders, and the chickadees, redpolls and blue jays stencilled little stars and sunbursts in the snow.

It is instinctive for predatory animals and humans to study the tracks of other animals, to hunt them or to learn their habits. It is also instinctive for most humans to want to cover their tracks. We like our activities to be private, but in February the snow is an open page where our comings and goings are recorded, not on the sands of time but for a brief period on the snows of yesterday.

Let It Be Remembered

When I read modern poetry, a lot of which I either do not understand or find depressing, I yearn for the return of poetry that sings, like Emily Dickinson's,

> I taste a liquor never brewed
> From tankards scooped in pearl;
> Not all the vats upon the Rhine
> Yield such an alcohol!

or Sara Teasdale's "Let it be forgotten, as a flower is forgotten/Forgotten as a fire that once was singing gold."

Even if you didn't understand English you could hear the music. And if you do understand English the words leave an imprint that is easily remembered.

Remembering becomes a large part of your consciousness as you grow older. Proust was prematurely mature in his remembrance of things past, but all of us can clearly remember small details from our childhood—the smell of a certain bakery, the silky touch of fine dust between bare toes on a country road, the surprising blue of glacial ice. Do we remember childhood sensations so clearly because our five senses were less atrophied or was the sensory data bank in our small brains less crowded?

Instead of Sara Teasdale's "Let it be forgotten," I find "let it be remembered" more and more a part of my awareness. And I think a friend or family member bequeaths us the memory of things they said or did or cared about. Some are funny. Some are beautiful and some just pop into your mind uninvited because the situation invokes them.

When I am driving behind an unusually slow driver or an enormous truck spewing diesel fumes and the annoying vehicle finally turns off the road, I invariably remember my father's triumphant shout, "Another Indian bit the dust!" I never chop an onion without recalling my mother-in-law's instruction to "shiver up an onion."

Louise Andrews Kent, better known as Mrs. Appleyard, was a wonderfully entertaining and versatile lady, writer, gourmet cook, musician, lecturer, and furnisher of miniature houses. But what do I do in remembrance of her? Every time I toss a salad I am honor bound to turn it twenty-one times, not twenty, twenty-two, but twenty-one because she suggested it. This would have amused her because she cared more about her guests than the exact number of times a salad was tossed.

Gladys Taber, one of the nicest people I never met except through her books, had the facility of choosing the precise word in description. She spoke of baby pheasants "twinkling across the road" behind their mother. I find that she has bequeathed phrases and insights to me, and though I never consciously imitate Mrs. Kent, Mrs. Taber, Robert Frost, or Emily Dickinson, it is inevitable that they have influenced my style of writing by their delight in the carefully-chosen word.

I never plant morning glory seeds, those little ebony chunks, without remembering how much my sister loved her Heavenly Blues. And when ours finally bloom, too near the date of our first fall frost, she is there enjoying them with me.

There will be some "things" we will leave to our children, not silver (most of that was stolen), not jewels or priceless antiques (we never had either), but the things we cared about. I doubt if they will ever feed a pig, cradle a chicken under their arm or attack the weeds in a garden without remembering me. What I hope for in the way of immortality is that our two daughters and three little grandsons will come upon a beaver in a pond, pick the first new peas, find the exact word to make a color or taste live on the page and that they will do this, "in remembrance of me."

CHRISTIAN HERALD
People Making A Difference

Christian Herald is a family of dedicated, Christ-centered ministries that reaches out to deprived children in need, and to homeless men who are lost in alcoholism and drug addiction. Christian Herald also offers the finest in family and evangelical literature through its book clubs and publishes a popular, dynamic magazine for today's Christians.

Our Ministries

Family Bookshelf and **Christian Bookshelf** provide a wide selection of inspirational reading and Christian literature written by best-selling authors. All books are recommended by an Advisory Board of distinguished writers and editors.

Christian Herald magazine is contemporary, a dynamic publication that addresses the vital concerns of today's Christian. Each monthly issue contains a sharing of true personal stories written by people who have found in Christ the strength to make a difference in the world around them.

Christian Herald Children. The door of God's grace opens wide to give impoverished youngsters a breath of fresh air, away from the evils of the streets. Every summer, hundreds of youngsters are welcomed at the Christian Herald Mont Lawn Camp located in the Poconos at Bushkill, Pennsylvania. Year-round assistance is also provided, including teen programs, tutoring in reading and writing, family counseling, career guidance and college scholarship programs.

The Bowery Mission. Located in New York City, the Bowery Mission offers hope and Gospel strength to the downtrodden and homeless. Here, the men of Skid Row are fed, clothed, ministered to. Many voluntarily enter a 6-month discipleship program of spiritual guidance, nutrition therapy and Bible study.

Our Father's House. Located in rural Pennsylvania, Our Father's House is a discipleship and job training center. Alcoholics and drug addicts are given an opportunity to recover, away from the temptations of city streets.

Christian Herald ministries, founded in 1878, are supported by the voluntary contributions of individuals and by legacies and bequests. Contributions are tax deductible. Checks should be made out to Christian Herald Children, The Bowery Mission, or to Christian Herald Association.

Administrative Office: 40 Overlook Drive, Chappaqua, New York 10514
Telephone: (914) 769-9000

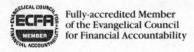

Fully-accredited Member
of the Evangelical Council
for Financial Accountability